A SECOND

MENSA

PUZZLE BOOK

A SECOND

MENSA
PUZZLE BOOK

VICTOR SEREBRIAKOFF
HONORARY INTERNATIONAL PRESIDENT OF MENSA

CHANCELLOR
PRESS

First published in Great Britain in 1993 by Chancellor Press
an imprint of Reed Consumer Books Limited
Michelin House, 81 Fulham Road, London SW3 6RB
and Auckland, Melbourne, Singapore and Toronto

Copyright © 1993 Victor Serebriakoff

ISBN 1 85152 384 7

A CIP catalogue record for this book is available
at the British Library

Typeset by DCF Enterprises
Printed in Great Britain by Bath Press

CONTENTS

Acknowledgments

My first acknowledgment must be to the hundreds of Mensa members who have exchanged puzzle ideas with me for forty years or so.

Particularly, I thank Mr Harold Gale, the Executive Director of British Mensa for his help in many ways, Mr Kenneth Russell who runs the puzzle page in the British Mensa Magazine and has helped me a lot and Dr Abbie Salny, Psychological Adviser to Mensa International and a great puzzle expert.

Thanks also to my wife Win, my son Mark, my daughter Judith and my daughter-in-law Elizabeth, as well as my grand-daughter Alexandra who has inspired some of the puzzles. I thank Sir Clive Sinclair, Chairman of British Mensa, for setting me off on puzzle composing some years ago.

I CONFESS

As I said about my first *Mensa Puzzle Book*, I sin and I know that I sin. Giving people more problems than they have already in these uncertain times is bad enough, but when they are invented problems that do not need to be solved it is downright unsocial. To distract the intelligent, for they are the ones who are hooked on puzzles, from their own and the world's problems is unworthy work for an old man, who could use his own ability better than to divert other able people from the struggle with reality that urgently requires their full attention.

If that were all! I sin, and I do not grieve for or regret my sin. Much worse, I take a sadistic, wicked pleasure in posing tricky, devious mindcrackers to thwart and mystify my helpless puzzle-addicted readers.

I presumptuously offer you this chance, at the beginning, to draw back from my challenge, because I know from experience that most will ignore my warning. Listening to the amoral voice of the market, the sales of my earlier puzzle books, I guess that my fair warning will discourage few but will challenge and stimulate most. So be it!

You have been warned. You asked for it. Abandon all hope, ye who turn these pages. You will spend hours of mindbending solitary mental labour for little but the satisfaction of solving some of my teasers. I wish you great success. No, let me be honest, I wish you just enough success to keep you trying!

There is one thing that worries me. Nothing is entirely good or evil. I have this fear that in offering you the indulgence and the mind-sharpening practice of a couple of hundred mindstretchers, which unlike real-life problems do have clear and definite answers, I may be doing good. There is the risk that those with mental talent but with insufficient faith in themselves may gain confidence and, by mental exercise and practice, become better at real problems. What greater failure can there be than to set out to hurt and merely help. I will not think about it. Doing good by stealth is all very well, but doing good while intending harm is quite another matter.

Victor Serebriakoff
January 1993

ABOUT THE PUZZLES

As a further diversion to the main types of puzzle, I am including a simple version of the first game I ever composed for a computer. In that game, the letters of a well-known phrase were revealed one at a time on the screen in their correct position. As soon as the player recognised the incomplete phrase he stopped the programme and was told how many points had been earned. The sooner the phrase was correctly guessed, the more points were scored.

The version included in this book is similar. At the bottom of most right-hand pages will be found a box, in which some of the letters of a well-known phrase appear in their correct position. As you turn over to the next page a few more letters are added, until after about five pages the complete phrase is shown . The aim is to spot the phrase with the fewest possible letters displayed. If you can identify the phrase from fewer than 20% of its letters that, I grudgingly admit, is very good. If you need 75% of the letters you are – a good trier.

All the remaining puzzles have a unique answer number. The answers, which are grouped together at the back of the book, are in a different order from the puzzles. This prevents involuntary peeking at the next answer before you come to that puzzle. A cross-reference to the puzzle number is included with the answer, in case you become so engrossed in the answer that you forget the number of the puzzle whose answer you are checking.

MENSA

To be a Mensa member is to be a certified puzzle solver. We are, we Mensans, the whole lot of us dedicated, masochistic, puzzle fiends. Our hundreds of journals, international, national and local, are full of nasty, tricky, unhelpful, devious puzzles, posers, enigmas, quizzes and problems. It has been calculated that the brain-hours we 103,000 Mensans devote each year to puzzles would, if we could ever agree on anything and turn our minds to systematic cooperation, solve all the world's social, political, economic and cultural problems – and produce a world of excruciatingly boring perfection. The need for interesting puzzles would increase a thousand-fold!

However, Mensa has no dogma. Fortunately, we agree on nothing except that we delight in each other's provoking, stimulating company. So we shall continue to throw up, as we should, a wide variety of views, ideas, proposals and hypotheses for general acceptance or rejection.

Perhaps you would like to know more about this odd bunch.

What is Mensa?

Mensa is a unique society. It is, basically, a social club – but a social club different from others. The only qualification for membership is a high score on an intelligence test. One person in fifty should qualify for membership; these people will come from all walks of life and have a wide variety of interests and occupations.

Mensa is the Latin word for table: we are a round-table society where no one has special precedence. We fill a void for many intelligent people otherwise cut off from contact with other good minds – contact that is important to them, but elusive in modern society. Besides being an origin of many new friendships, we provide members with a receptive but critical audience on which to try out new ideas.

Mensa is protean: its most visible feature is its diversity. It crosses the often artificial barriers which separate people from each other. It recruits, not like other societies by persuading people to think as they do, but by scientifically selecting people who are able to think for themselves. Yet, although there appears to be little common ground and little surface agreement between members, we find there is an underlying unity which gives an unexpected strength to the society.

Mensa has three aims: social contact between intelligent people; research in psychology and the social sciences; and the identification and fostering of human intelligence. Mensa is an international society; it has over 100,000 members in over 100 countries. We have members of almost every occupation – businessmen, clerks, doctors, editors, factory workers, farm labourers, housewives, lawyers, policemen, politicians, soldiers, scientists, students, teachers are just some examples – and of every age from young children to octogenarian such as myself.

The Mensa Preliminary I.Q. Test

If you do well in these dreadful puzzles you are probably eligible to join Mensa. Or perhaps you would in any case like to know your I.Q. Be it understood that a really valid measurement of intelligence quotient can only be obtained from an approved test administered under standard conditions by a trained psychologist or test administrator. However, Mensa usually sends an informal do-it-yourself test to applicants to help them to judge if it is worth their while to attend one of our many supervised test sessions around the country. These home tests, we find, give a very good first approximation of I.Q.

By arrangement with British Mensa, I have included one of these Mensa Preliminary Tests in this book for you to try your hand at. Mensa have made a special offer to the publisher to mark this test for you for a concessionary fee of £5 in place of the normal fee of £9.75. This offer applies to readers in the U.K. and Eire only. Complete the answer sheets and detach them where indicated, send them with the £5 fee to Mensa and they will send you back within a day or two an estimate of how intelligent you are.

If you do well, you may then be offered the opportunity of the final supervised test and a chance to join over a hundred thousand of us as a member of the world-wide Clever Club of which I am honorary president. This is the first time a Mensa preliminary test has been offered in a book in this way.

If you want to do the test right away it will act as a warm up for the rigours of the puzzles themselves. Alternatively, you can leave it until the puzzles have sharpened your wits.

For further information about Mensa contact

British Mensa
Mensa House
St John's Square
Wolverhampton
WV2 4AH

International Mensa
15 The Ivories
6-8 Northampton Street
London
N1 2HV

THE I.Q. TEST

This is an *untimed* or *Power* Test, and it was designed to measure the higher levels of intelligence. This makes it impossible to standardize on the normal population and it was standardized on Mensa applicants, a highly selected sample. It must be taken for what it is worth. It has been keyed in to the test scores of those applicants and should provide a fairly good guide at the upper levels. Although designed to test high cognitive ability, it has questions of graded difficulty. Everyone should be able to start each test but very few should be able to finish any of them. The question is not 'Can you finish?' but 'How far can you get?'.

The battery comprises seven tests, each probing different abilities. You will be allowed as much time as you like.

Go through each test in order. Do not hurry. Read each question carefully and go ahead at a fast but comfortable speed. Do not waste too much time if you are stumped – pass on and come back to that question later. It is worthwhile to guess if you do not think you can answer surely.

When you have finished all seven tests transfer the answers to the answer sheet which immediately follows them. Detach it from the book and post it with the £5 fee to:

British Mensa
Mensa House
St John's Square
Wolverhampton
WV2 4AH

TEST 1: Find the odd one out

Test 1 is aimed at testing the most important human ability, classification, the supreme trick of conceptual intelligence which collects things into named mental slots to help thinking.

Here you are given five words. You have to think about the various ways of classifying them. Some ways of looking at them leave one of them out, the 'odd one out'. There is one simple, fairly obvious way, the other ways are obscure or tortuous. You have to find the odd one out by the simplest rule. There is a quality or attribute which four of the words in each question share which is not shared by the odd one out.

Underline the word whose meaning does not fit in with the others, the odd one out.

Example: knife, fork, spoon, hat, cup.
Answer: hat – the others are tableware.

 (1) A bird, B plane, C bee, D car, E butterfly
 (2) A look, B glance, C stare, D wink, E observe
 (3) A rain, B snow, C sleet, D lightning, E hail
 (4) A cotton, B wool, C nylon, D flax, E silk
 (5) A lifeless, B languid, C torpid, D numb, E sensitive
 (6) A throw, B kick, C hurl, D toss, E pitch
 (7) A beech, B ash, C spruce, D willow, E sycamore
 (8) A cerise, B scarlet, C magenta, D crimson, E saffron
 (9) A gelding, B bitch, C doe, D ewe, E filly
(10) A distemper, B anthrax, C martingale, D spavin,
      E rinderpest
(11) A dignified, B stately, C sublime, D august, E grand
(12) A pearl, B agate, C sapphire, D emerald, E ruby
(13) A funambulist, B acrobat, C clown, D fool, E virago
(14) A triturate, B powder, C granulate, D titrate, E pulverize
(15) A daffodil, B tulip, C snowdrop, D chrysanthemum,
      E gladiolus

TEST 2: Words which mean the same

This tests your comprehension of language. There are six words in each question, and two of the words are closer in meaning than any other pair. Find the two words which mean nearly the same and underline them.

Example: walk, run, drive, stroll, fly, sit
Answer: 'walk' and 'stroll' are closest in meaning.

(1) A soon, B almost, C nearly, D partly, E often, F portion
(2) A forgo, B forget, C detest, D leave, E possess, F abhor
(3) A inhuman, B brutal, C manly, D careful,
     E compassionate, F celestial
(4) A ill, B peculiar, C odd, D weary, E stilted, F funny
(5) A ghostly, B gruesome, C comely, D thin, E horrible,
     F tasteless
(6) A wanton, B mediocre, C repulsive, D absurd,
     E ludicrous, F meaningful
(7) A everything, B blended, C many, D main, E complete,
     F entire
(8) A befriended, B watched, C fetched, D escorted,
     E accompanied, F joined
(9) A combat, B fulfil, C oppose, D exist, E affect, F apply
(10) A resistance, B allowance, C reason, D impedance,
     E affliction, F effect
(11) A relevant, B saucy, C absurd, D pertinent, E impatient,
     F intrusive
(12) A afternoon, B countryside, C gloaming, D daytime,
     E heathland, F twilight
(13) A pettifog, B quibble, C render, D assist, E demonstrate
     F destroy
(14) A iambic, B obscene, C perverse, D wayward, E mean,
     F argumentative
(15) A hat, B split, C manager, D stable, E dubious, F trifid

TEST 3: Opposites

This is again a test of clear conceptual comprehension and grasp of meaning. Two of the words in each question mean more exactly the opposite of each other than any other pair. They mean the reverse of each other. Find the two 'opposites' and underline them.

Example: curved, long, big, small, broad
Answer: 'big' and 'small' are the most opposite

(1) A rotate, B ascent, C plunge, D approach, E descent
(2) A leak, B withdraw, C overflow, D approach, E escape
(3) A derail, B unsettle, C float, D dislodge, E sink
(4) A calm, B inactive, C relaxed, D employed, E numbed
(5) A sever, B wrench, C unseat, D join, E pluck
(6) A bluff, B blunt, C hard, D stinging, E acute
(7) A operatic, B discordant, C cantabile, D syncopation,
     E melodic
(8) A think, B learn, C calculate, D forego, E forget
(9) A filibuster, B opportunist, C assailant, D adversary,
     F partner
(10) A meagre, B fluent, C mean, D superfluous, E copious
(11) A alive, B dull, C slothful, D inert, E bemused
(12) A detach, B rally, C scatter, D debunk, E enthuse
(13) A patriotic, B animated, C seditious, D agitated,
     E motivated
(14) A toddler, B flapper, C stripling, D adolescent, E dotard
(15) A silky, B unshaven, C suave, D rounded, E coarse
(16) A loosen, B pay, C demand, D receive, E invoice
(17) A peccable, B seedy, C honoured, D saintly, E loving
(18) A cummerbund, B sash, C bandolier, D peruke, F buskin
(19) A stocky, B homunculus, C stubby, D giant, E squat

TEST 4: Add on words

This is a test of how well your mind works in scan and recall. It checks how well ordered your mental filing system is. There is a word which fits on *after* the first word to make another word. Also the word you are seeking fits on *before* the second word to make another sensible word. The number of hyphens tells you how many letters are missing. Sometimes a letter or two of the missing word is given as a clue. Write in the missing letters above the hyphens so as to make up the missing word.

Example: house *hold* all

(1)	green	_ _ _ _ _	wife
(2)	letter	p _ _ _ s	ups
(3)	pin	t _ _ _ e	cloth
(4)	broad	c _ _ _	away
(5)	fly	w _ _ _ _	wright
(6)	pick	_ _ _ _ _ _	book
(7)	pad	_ _ _ k	smith
(8)	leader	_ _ _ _	mate
(9)	with	_ _ _ _	all
(10)	spin	d _ _ _ t	wood
(11)	farm	_ _ _ _ _	fast
(12)	mud	_ _ _ k	spur
(13)	honey	_ _ _ _	light
(14)	dung	_ _ _ _	top
(15)	wood	_ _ _ _ _ _	hole
(16)	flame	_ _ _ _ _	reader
(17)	inter	_ _ _ _	thing

TEST 5: Double meanings

This tests similar abilities to Test 4. Find the middle word. You are looking for a word which has the same meaning as the first word *in one sense* and the same meaning as the second word *in another sense*. Fill in the missing letters. Some are already shown as a clue.

Example: breathes heavily _ a _ _ _ underclothes
Answer: 'pants' because to breathe heavily is to pant and pants are also underclothes.

(1)	creep	– – e – –	rob
(2)	look	_ _ _ _ _	time-piece
(3)	pound	_ _ _ _	patrol
(4)	hyphen	d _ _ _	run
(5)	learn	_ _ _ _ y	room
(6)	lose	_ _ _ _	hut
(7)	waste	_ _ _ _ s _	deny
(8)	wilderness	_ _ _ _ _ _	leave
(9)	flop	_ _ _ _ _ _ _ r	fish
(10)	climb	_ _ _ _ _	horse
(11)	heave	_ _ _ _ h	tar
(12)	vulgar	_ _ _ _ _ _	heath
(13)	lots	_ _ _ _ _ _ _	books
(14)	black	_ _ _ _ _	bird
(15)	saffron	_ _ _ _ _	fruit
(16)	teacher	_ o _ _ _	charabanc
(17)	maw	_ _ _ _ h	voice
(18)	nincompoop	b _ _ _ _	bird
(19)	component	_ _ _ _ _ _	agent

TEST 6: Completion

Here we are testing comprehension and your sense of the appropriate. There are three incomplete sentences. You are offered five alternative words for each space left vacant. The task is to find the most *appropriate* word for each space. You are looking for the *combination* that best fits so as to make sense. Write the letter which is in front of the correct word in each space.

Completion

Complete the quotations from the selection of words shown in the *Alternatives* given below.

I want to go . . . . 1 . . . . from the . . . . 2 . . . ., where the . . . . 3 . . . .
doesn't crouch over me like a . . . . 4 . . . . waiting to . . . . 5 . . . . .

The . . . . 6 . . . . genius is a . . . . 7 . . . . of large . . . . 8 . . . . powers,
. . . . 9 . . . . determined to some . . . . 10 . . . . direction.

The . . . . 11 . . . . of . . . . 12 . . . . constitution are . . . 13 . . . . lost
when the . . . . 14 . . . . power is . . . . 15 . . . . by the executive.

Alternatives

(1) A near, B east, C far, D west, E pontificating
(2) A hurricane, B winter, C tornado, D lightning, E thunder
(3) A cold, B desert, C heat, D heavens, E stars
(4) A mouse, B stag, C mole, D snow-leopard, E rabbit
(5) A pounce, B stagger, C rush, D sleep, E forget
(6) A lost, B missing, C evil, D true, E desperate
(7) A mind, B thought, C charge, D wave, E spread

24

(8) A general, B overt, C bland, D changed, E altered
(9) A separately, B accidentally, C fondly, D tentatively, E haltingly
(10) A lost, B particular, C piscatorial, D mythological, E rosy
(11) A kernels, B principles, C personalities, D principals, E imagination
(12) A autonomous, B chartered, C licensed, D free, E effortless
(13) A irrevocably, B indispensably, C imperatively, D spontaneously, E awkwardly
(14) A legislative, B codification, C chartered, D consultative, E spasmodic
(15) A accredited, B usurped, C deputed, D cured, E accepted

TEST 7: Problems

Now comes the crunch. This is where we sort out the men from the boys (or the women from the girls).

If you reach these questions undiscouraged, good! They are meant to discriminate among the top dogs. There are ten tricky questions which test your logical powers, your memory, comprehension and your quickness on your mental feet. Watch out for catches.

Again you are given a number of alternative answers to choose from. Write down the letter of the correct answer in the space provided in the table overleaf.

Problems

(1) A man purchased a car for £650 and sold it for £725. He was then told that he had sold too cheaply, so he bought the car back for £750 but could sell it for only £725. How much profit or loss had he made?

(2) Mr Allen has a green door, Mr Ball does not have a red door, Mr Clark has a white door if Mr Ball has a red door, Mr Doe has a black door if Mr Allen has a green door, Mr Edge has a red door. Which one of these statements might be true?
   (A) Mr Allen has a red door.
   (B) Mr Ball has a white door.
   (C) Mr Clark has a white door.
   (D) Mr Doe has a black door.
   (E) Mr Edge has a black door.

(3) A frog is at the bottom of a 30ft deep well. He climbs up 3ft and slips back 2ft each day. How many days will it take him to reach the top?

(4) One man's watch showed 6.10, another 6.25, another 6.40, yet another 6.55. If the correct time was 6.30, what was the average amount of time fast or slow that showed on all the watches?

(5) A boat is anchored in the harbour, and over its side is a rope-ladder with the last rung just touching the water. The rungs are 200mm apart. When the tide comes in it rises 1600mm. How many rungs are covered?

26

(6) A man bought a number of eggs at a shop. $^2/_3$ were cracked, $^1/_2$ were bad, $^1/_4$ were both cracked and bad, 2 were O.K. How many eggs did the man buy?

(7) A cyclist cycles 10 miles to town A at 4 miles per hour. He does the return journey at 6 miles per hour. How many minutes does he take to do both journeys?

(8) A factory owner decided to give each of his employees a bonus. As he was a chauvinist he decided to give each man £1 and each woman 40p. Then he had second thoughts. As he had 1000 employees it would cost too much even though there were more women than men. He would wait until 60% of the men were away on a course and give the bonus only to those remaining. How much did it cost him?

(9) In a Sports Centre 70% play squash, 75% play tennis, 80% play badminton, 85% play table-tennis. What is the minimum percentage that play all four sports?

(10) A man has 3 white socks, 3 black socks, 3 pink socks and 3 blue socks in his drawer. What is the minimum number of socks he must take out of the drawer to make up 3 pairs, assuming that he cannot see the colours?

Alternative answers   *Your answer*

(1) A loss £50, B loss £25, C nil, D profit £25,
     E profit £50   ....

(2) A, B, C, D, E   ....

(3) A 27, B 28, C 29, D 30, E 31   ....

(4) A 2$^1/_2$ mins slow, B 5 mins slow, C 10 mins fast,
     D 5 mins fast, E 7$^1/_2$ mins fast   ....

(5) A 9, B 8, C 7, D 6, E 0   ....

(6) A 24, B 36, C 48, D 60, E 72   ....

(7) A 220 mins, B 230 mins, C 240 mins, D 250 mins,
     E 260 mins   ....

(8) A £400, B £500, C £600, D £700, E £140   ....

(9) A 10%, B 15%, C 20%, D 25%, E 30%   ....

(10) A 6, B 7, C 8, D 9, E 10   ....

A SECOND MENSA PUZZLE BOOK
PRELIMINARY I.Q. TEST

Set out below are my answers to the seven tests. Please mark them and let me know my Intelligence Quotient as indicated by these tests. I understand that this will be only a rough approximation, and that it will be necessary to undertake a supervised test under standard conditions to obtain an accurate indication of I.Q.

I enlcose a cheque/postal order for £5. I am over 18 years old.

Name ....

Address ....

....

....

TEST ONE *(circle the letter signifying your answer)*

1	A	B	C	D	E	9	A	B	C	D	E
2	A	B	C	D	E	10	A	B	C	D	E
3	A	B	C	D	E	11	A	B	C	D	E
4	A	B	C	D	E	12	A	B	C	D	E
5	A	B	C	D	E	13	A	B	C	D	E
6	A	B	C	D	E	14	A	B	C	D	E
7	A	B	C	D	E	15	A	B	C	D	E
8	A	B	C	D	E						

TEST TWO *(circle the two letters comprising your answer)*

1	A	B	C	D	E	F	9	A	B	C	D	E	F
2	A	B	C	D	E	F	10	A	B	C	D	E	F
3	A	B	C	D	E	F	11	A	B	C	D	E	F
4	A	B	C	D	E	F	12	A	B	C	D	E	F
5	A	B	C	D	E	F	13	A	B	C	D	E	F
6	A	B	C	D	E	F	14	A	B	C	D	E	F
7	A	B	C	D	E	F	15	A	B	C	D	E	F
8	A	B	C	D	E								

TEST THREE *(circle the two letters comprising your answer)*

1	A	B	C	D	E	11	A	B	C	D	E
2	A	B	C	D	E	12	A	B	C	D	E
3	A	B	C	D	E	13	A	B	C	D	E
4	A	B	C	D	E	14	A	B	C	D	E
5	A	B	C	D	E	15	A	B	C	D	E
6	A	B	C	D	E	16	A	B	C	D	E
7	A	B	C	D	E	17	A	B	C	D	E
8	A	B	C	D	E	18	A	B	C	D	E
9	A	B	C	D	E	19	A	B	C	D	E
10	A	B	C	D	E						

TEST FOUR *(write in the missing word)*

1 ....
2 ....
3 ....
4 ....
5 ....
6 ....
7 ....
8 ....
9 ....

10 ....
11 ....
12 ....
13 ....
14 ....
15 ....
16 ....
17 ....

TEST FIVE *(write in the missing word)*

1 ....
2 ....
3 ....
4 ....
5 ....
6 ....
7 ....
8 ....
9 ....
10 ....

11 ....
12 ....
13 ....
14 ....
15 ....
16 ....
17 ....
18 ....
19 ....

TEST SIX *(circle the letter signifying your choice of word)*

1	A	B	C	D	E	9	A	B	C	D	E
2	A	B	C	D	E	10	A	B	C	D	E
3	A	B	C	D	E	11	A	B	C	D	E
4	A	B	C	D	E	12	A	B	C	D	E
5	A	B	C	D	E	13	A	B	C	D	E
6	A	B	C	D	E	14	A	B	C	D	E
7	A	B	C	D	E	15	A	B	C	D	E
8	A	B	C	D	E						

TEST SEVEN *(circle the letter indicating your answer)*

1	A	B	C	D	E	6	A	B	C	D	E
2	A	B	C	D	E	7	A	B	C	D	E
3	A	B	C	D	E	8	A	B	C	D	E
4	A	B	C	D	E	9	A	B	C	D	E
5	A	B	C	D	E	10	A	B	C	D	E

Send the complete answer sheets
with the special £5 marking fee to:
BRITISH MENSA
Mensa House
St John's Square
Wolverhampton
WV2 4AH

THE PUZZLES

Q1. The quality of quality control

Mr Poker, the quality control inspector at a factory, is worried. In front of him are twelve bins of spigolated grotchets, all exactly the same in appearance. But alarmingly, the foundry manager has reported that an ingot of bolenium alloy is missing and he suspects that one of the twelve batches may have been cast from that, instead of from the refridium alloy as it should have been. The result would be catastrophic. The assembled moltagating turbolators using the overweight grotchet would desontify completely.

Now as every readers knows, bolenium alloy is 1.23% more dense than refridium alloy, and the inspector only has to weigh a grotchet from each bin to find the faulty bin. The faulty grotchet would weigh 24.3 milligrams more than those from the good bins. Mr Poker therefore told his nervous, newly engaged assistant, Caroline, to weigh one from each batch and report back. 'Hurry,' he said. 'It's urgent.'

Two minutes later Caroline brought him a sample from the faulty batch.

'Batch eleven. Here is one of them,' she said, 'just 24.3 milligrams heavier.'

'Foolish girl,' he said. 'No-one, not even a starter like you, could do twelve weighings in that time. Go back and weigh them properly.'

'But, Sir, if you please, there was no need for twelve weighings.'

'You must learn not to argue if you want to keep this job. Go back and do as you are told.'

Caroline came back in an hour having dutifully obeyed instructions,

'So which batch was it really?' asked Mr Poker.

'Eleven, Sir.'

Mr Poker looked cross. He weighed the first and second

E   E E E   E E
  E E E E   E

samples himself and one from another bin. 'Lucky guess,' he said. 'The girl will not do; she is unreliable.'

Caroline was on a one day trial. She was told that she was unsuitable at the end of the day. 'In inspection you simply cannot use arm-chancers,' Mr Poker told his boss.

Was he being just? Could the job be done with less than twelve weighings? If so, what is the fewest number?

Answer 11

Q2. Mathematical flirtation ✓

Professor Cornelius Kalkalus met Lady Pamela Swot at the Higher Purer Mathematics Congress. Despite his scruffy beard and her great height and cruel wit they were attracted to each other and began to flirt obscurely.

After quarrelling about Carnap for a time, he became personal. 'How old are you, — Pamela, may I call you that?'
'I shan't tell you and No, respectively.'
'Go on. Give me a clue!'
'No.'
'Do.'
'On no account.'
When he walked away she scribbled the design below on her card. She went across and dropped it at his feet, turned on her heel, and walked away.

The professor took a minute to solve it, joined her and said, 'Well, I'm forty, Pamela. Shall we take a risk with that trifle?'

'If there's nothing more appetizing,' she responded, and took his arm.

How old was Pamela?

Answer 22

1	2	3
1	5	21
8	13	?

←

36

Q3. Poles apart together

When I was nineteen, Georgie and I did a bit of labouring. We were erecting a fence for a new timber yard, using six foot lengths of second-hand telegraph poles as fenceposts. It was overtime, Sunday work, and no one actually works on overtime when the foreman is not there, do they? So we were messing about. Which was much harder than working, actually.

'What is the greatest number of poles which you can arrange so that each one touches all the others?' I challenged. Georgie and I laboured for about an hour until we came to an answer.

We easily got four to be mutually touching, and then I thought of a way to get more. We tried it and it worked, but that was when the foreman came by on his way to the pub. We got the sack – again. We seemed to get sacked several times each week.

In the pub later Georgie thought of a way to have even more poles with each touching all the others. I swore it wouldn't work. We bet a pint on it. The foreman was there and he agreed with me. He bet a pint on my side.

So when we were thrown out of the pub, we all went back to the site and started pole heaving. Georgie cheered and sang with joy and I cursed when his ridiculous cheating method worked out and he got one more than I had to be mutually touching. The foreman laughed and promised to pay. He was very drunk!

It was three in the morning, and the neighbours were shouting at us from their windows. So we went to a pub we knew where the landlord was friendly, and whose clock had stopped. The foreman and I bought Georgie his pints, but he was sick and we almost carried him home. The foreman said something very hard to hear. I think he said that if we were late next day we would get the sack.

How many poles did I get mutually touching? How many did Georgie? Why were we and the foreman such fools?

Answer 33

```
EM  E   E   E       E   E
 E ME   E   E           E
```

Q4. Three dice †

Harold and Cecil are playing with three ordinary dice. Cecil turns his back and gives these orders.

'Throw the dice. Don't tell me how they fall.'

Three dice are rolled. They fall as 6, 4 and 1.

'Total the top numbers, but do not tell me the answer. Now pick any dice, add the bottom number to your total, throw that dice again and add its top number to your total.'

Cecil turns round and finds the dice lying 5, 6 and 4. 'Your grand total is 22,' he says.

How did he know?

Answer 44

Q5. Puzzle for life

Bug-eyed alien monsters have invaded the earth and subdued humanity. They are selecting the most intelligent humans by posing problems. Those that solve them survive as well treated, even cosseted, slaves. The rest are disposed of.

You are locked in a blank-walled concrete cell, with light and ventilation well out of your reach. You are stark naked. You are taken away for meals by a robot. The cell has a hole in the floor about 50mm across – too small to get your hand in – and 200mm deep. At the bottom of the hole you can see the tantalising sight of the key to the cell door attached to a rubber ball. If you escape you establish your right to live. There is nothing in the cell except you, and the air you breathe. Don't think you can smuggle anything in; every time you enter the cell you are checked with great care by the hyper-intelligent robots of the aliens. You want to live, even if it means being a slave.

How do you get the key and save your life?

Answer 55

Q6. Getting serious about series

Lady Pamela Swot wrote these three numbers on the blackboard — 1, 3, 8.

She stared over her pince-nez at Professor Kalkalus, Corny as she called him.

'Corny, dear, you are so quick and clever. What is there odd about these three integers?'

'Oh! Lots of things, Pam dear, but I suppose you are looking at something quite obvious and trivial.'

'Try not to be offensive, Corny, it makes you unlovable.'

'Lovable, alas, I can never be. But I'll compose a poem to please you.'

> The product of any pair,
> Is one short of a square.

'Irritating man. Why can't you learn the charm of being cleverly wrong sometimes. Now this is the real test. Can you add another number to the series without breaking the rule in your disgusting bit of doggerel?'

Corny figured on paper for a time and gave her an answer.

'How wretched. I thought you'd take a day.'

'And do you know yet another integer in that series, Pamela?'

'Goodness, no! Is there one? There can't be. You are deceiving me. How cruel!'

What was the number the professor found, the fourth in the series? Was there a fifth in the series, and if so what was it?

Answer 66

<table>
<tr><td>E M</td><td>RE</td><td>E</td><td>RE</td><td></td><td>E</td><td>ER</td></tr>
<tr><td>E MERR</td><td>ER</td><td>E</td><td></td><td></td><td>E</td><td></td></tr>
</table>

Q7. Classifying clouds

Tommy and Teddy were in the Special Needs class because they were much too clever, and got bored. This made them lazy and sometimes disruptively cheeky in class.

The special needs class was a small room, away from other students, where they could read, study on their own, play with a computer and do whatever they liked, so long as they got out of their teacher's hair with their awkward questions and their bad behaviour.

It was a lovely summer's day, and Tommy looked longingly out of the window at the sky as he daydreamed. Then he started sketching and showed Teddy this picture of the clouds he had seen.

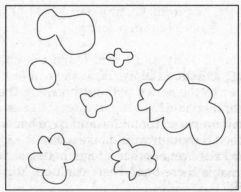

Tommy said, 'Those clouds are out of order. Bet you can't find the principle and explain their proper order.'

Teddy put down his comic and set to work. It took him ten minutes. 'Why do you say 'the' principle?' he asked. Then they argued a bit and came to a conclusion. What was it?

Answer 77

Q8. Little to help you

The next intelligence test devised by the aliens is this. You are taken to a room with many other candidates. Each is handcuffed naked at a separate small table on which are arranged the six wooden objects show below. You are given no instructions, but the word is around that if you can place them in the right order you will survive.

In what order across the table should they be arranged?

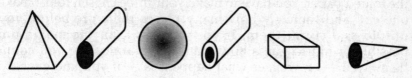

Answer 88

Q9. Bring back the magic

A magic square is one where the numbers in each cell add up to the same total down each column, across each row, and along the two diagonals. I have taken the magic out of the square on the left by rearranging the numbers according to a plan. You must recreate the magic in the blank square and identify the method I used to jumble the figures.

4	3	14	9
17	8	7	13
6	12	11	2
10	5	16	15

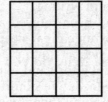

Answer 99

E M RE   E ARE   E   ER
E MERR ER   ES A   E

41

Q10. Can you cut free?

The number of human survivors is diminishing now. A fully qualified human slave of the aliens explains. He is a frightened young Scottish student who is on probation, and his voice tends to squeak from fear.

'You each get a sheet of A4 paper and a pair of scissors. You have to fold the paper just three times. The aim is to get the largest number of pieces by making a single straight cut across the folded paper. You have to make your three chosen folds, make one cut, and then say how many pieces there are before you unfold and count them. If you get less than the maximum possible or fail to guess how many there are before you count them, well — er, well, er what happens is — if you know what I mean. Er, er, it's over quickly, it doesn't hurt, er, I hope.'

How do you do it? And how many pieces can you make?

Answer 10

Q11. How to move sleepers

Georgie and I, after four more sackings, were still on site. We had completed the fence and were laying a wooden road for the timber yard. The road was made of railway sleepers which, being impregnated with creosote, were too heavy to lift – for us, anyway. Labouring had not been our game; we were better at reading and writing.

We had been refused a barrow, and there was nothing on site but those huge great sleepers and a dozen short offcuts. We could shift the sleepers into place by rolling them, but it was very slow and a great effort, and our fingers began to bleed.

Between us we could just lift one end of a sleeper and we started moving them by shifting one end at a time, but it was too exhausting. Then we thought of a much better way to move them, without recourse to any other means than those already mentioned. What was it?

Answer 1

Q12. Classifying ✓

These hexagons seem all to be different, but some are more similar than others.

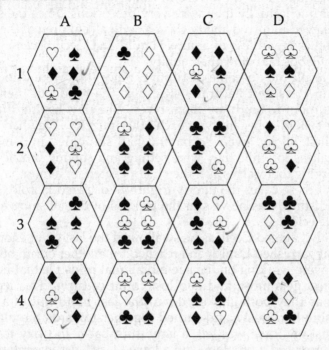

You are a taxonomist, whose job entails finding ways to classify objects. Faced with these sixteen hexagons, can you find any pairs that go together? The link may not be very obvious, but it does exist.

Make a note of the column and row number of any linking pairs that you can find.

Answer 12

THE MORE WE ARE TOGETHER
THE MERRIER WE SHALL BE

Q13. Gorging sickening pastries

Harold and Cecil were at a small but prestigious preparatory school. Emotionally they were normal mischievous eleven year olds, but intellectually they were very precocious. Since the school head believed in mixed ability classes, with all children of the same age together regardless of ability, Harold and Cecil became bored with a syllabus far below their ability.

As a result they became disruptive. Since they were difficult to handle in class, but naturally studious, the head put them in a separate room to study by themselves. One day, having finished their set task they began to set each other puzzles. They had made some illicit, sticky, sweet cocoa and had smuggled in some rich cream cakes. So while they were setting and solving puzzles they were gorging themselves as if they hadn't eaten for a month.

'Aren't these cakes too utterly frightful!' declared Harold, somewhat indistinctly as he was in the process of demolishing a large chocolate éclair.

'Ghastly!' agreed Cecil, as he swallowed the last of an enormous rich, fruit garnished Danish and reached for another cream bun.

They were working on the age-old animal principle that he who eats fastest gets most, and had lost count of turns. This led to a dispute as they both choked down the last mouthful of a large pastry simultaneously, and turned together towards the plate on which just one cake was left, a large rum baba. Too lazy to fight, Harold proposed a problem, and allowed Cecil just five minutes to solve it. If he succeeded he was to get the awful cake.

'Take these words:' said Harold. 'List one: fallacy, difficulty, follow, corrosion, manna, seller. List two: hullabaloo, better, paravane, immense, mutter. Only one of the words in list two could belong in list one. To get the last cake, which is it?'

Well then, which is it?

Answer 23

Q14. What is the rule?

Both Harold and Cecil, the two precocious swots, hated physical jerks. They forged sick notes to avoid PE, and went fishing for tiddlers in a pond they knew of. It was located on a lovely disused rubbish tip on which you could find fascinating ancient rubbish.

But having each filled a string-handled jam jar with stickle-backs, tadpoles and water-weed, they got bored and began to bet.

'It's my turn to set you a problem,' said Cecil. 'It's a list of words, and you have to find the connection. As soon as you get it, you supply the next word in the list. If it does not follow the rule, you carry all the tackle home and do both lots of homework. If you get it right before I say the tenth word, I carry the stuff and do the home-work.'

Harold objected. 'I have a chance to spot the rule in twelve words or no bet.' They argued for ten minutes, scuffled enjoyably for a bit among the ashes, dusted themselves down, and settled for eleven words.

Here is Cecil's list: actual, grab, cattle, dead, every, fluff, gap, push, ink, raj, king. That is all eleven words allowed.

Harold guessed 'hat' as the next word and failed. Reluctantly, therefore, I will give you a list which contains a single good candidate for the next word. But you could find a hundred more!

Which of these words continues the list, and what is the rule?

MONEY, SCOT, BEVEL, COMPUTER, HAT, SKIRT

Answer 34

O O A A A O O O

Q15. How to avoid mate

This is an old, somewhat twisted chess problem invented by Karl Fabel. You will see why there has been a lot of argument about it.

Roberto is a chess prodigy whose fame has reached the ears of the court of Echekia.

Now the King of Echekia has been persuaded that he is a genius at chess by Baron Kraft, the Royal Chess Master. The King wants the satisfaction of defeating the young prodigy and Kraft is ordered to summon him to court. Kraft gives the uncourtly and unmannered Roberto a few games himself, and he is horrified. The clumsy bumpkin defeats him – Baron Kraft, the Second Board of Echekia – easily and repeatedly.

Kraft is terrified. If the King learns of his defeats by Roberto he may be replaced. He stalls, but the King grows more interested and insistent.

So far Kraft has fixed things so that the King is never defeated. His opponents are warned that it would be death to win, so they put up a show then resign respectfully and are given a purse of gold. The Baron decides that the best way for him to avoid demotion is to allow Roberto to do the unthinkable and defeat the King. Then Kraft can accuse him of cheating and have him executed for disrespect for the Crown.

Overwhelmed by the surroundings of the royal court, Roberto is ill at ease. His situation is not improved by the constant tittering by sycophantic courtiers at his failures in courtly behaviour. But the King is amused and likes Roberto, if only as a novelty.

They come to the game, and the King confidently offers Roberto white to encourage him.

After an hour they have reached the critical position shown overleaf. As the game has progressed the King's moves have taken longer and longer to make, whilst Roberto's moves have been shorter and shorter. It is Roberto's move.

Roberto has noticed the King's growing wrath and is full of fear. He pauses before the obvious move. Then noticing something move above the King's head he looks up into the beautiful but frightened face of the King's daughter, Princess Satasha. She

is silently speaking to him. 'If you win, you die,' he lip-reads.

But what can he do? He must lose, but how? He has to find a move which avoids a mate in one of the Black King.

The inspiration comes, and he leans forward and moves the white . . . .

There are three questions for you to answer:

1. What move can Roberto make to avoid mate in one?
2. What appears to be odd about the position shown?
3. What logical explanation is there for this oddity?

Answer 45

S OFO A AFA O OF O R

47

Q16. Shrimpoas

My grand-daughter was two. I found her half buried under a great heap of books below a bookshelf which was close to floor level. She was laughing with joy, scrabbling the books out on to the floor as fast as she could.

'What are you doing, Alexandra?' I asked.

She could not talk much, but she knew. 'Making a mess,' she gleefully explained.

He baby life was a dreary round of learning order, where things should be, what may be touched, and what must not be touched. She was having a brief, utterly joyous, holiday from order as when the Lord of Misrule reigns. Clowning has the same motivation – a brief revolt from the tyranny of gravity.

There is in all of us a pleasure which we have to fight – that of disordering things. I have indulged this pleasure with some of the most treasured aphorisms which our world culture has produced. I have mixed and muddled and ruined the compact and economical treasures of wisdom from men of genius.

Yours is the task of clearing up after my vandalism, and restoring order out of disorder. 'Shrimpoas' is a word-anagram of 'aphorisms'. Below are three sentence-anagrams – mixed up aphorisms including their source or author. You have to rearrange the words into their original order.

1. ANYTHING AS KEPLER NATURE LITTLE AS USES POSSIBLE OF

2. LAWS NEVER OWN DA VINCI NATURE BREAKS HER

3. WHO CANNOT LOVE TO FLATTER MUST GOETHE LEARN HE

Answer 56

Q17. Help a deprived poem

Polly Titian, having been hounded from her cabinet office by the shrieking headlines of the tabloids and the sober reproof of the rest of the media, said this: 'The habit of knocking success in any form is now the main occupation of the 'mediacracy'. I refer to those who command our rulers, the media pundits and moguls to whom praise is pain and who now rule the nation.'

I wrote this doggerel in sympathy with Polly. However, I have left you to fill in the rhyming words at the end of each pair of lines.

You might think of better pairs but you have to guess mine.

INCOMPLETE VERSE

The Air that God did freely
We all must breathe that we may
Aerobic unobstructed
Ensureth Health, delayeth
But air that's forced through vocal
Deformed and tortured into
By being muddled up
Thy cheeks and throat and teeth and
Imposes such a gruesome
On epiglottis, tongue and
That I advise, nay more,
That thou forbear, belt up!
Be silent. Speak not. Hold thy
From birth till final dirge be

But wait! I had forgotten,
There's one exception, I
Unless thy sad and sorry
Shall be to meet and know and

S   OF ON   AN   A FA O   N OF   O   R

A monster of that horrid
Whose plans and ventures all
For verbal noise may be
And speech itself may well be
To castigate and put those
Who are admired around the
So, Speakers must be ever
Save where achievers may be
The Rule of Dumbness may be
To hurt and humble able

Answer 67

Q18. Building a magic cube

Magic squares add up across, down and diagonally to the same constant. Too easy! Let us move into the third dimension. What about a magic cube?

Imagine a cube built of three magic squares, each with nine boxes, giving a total of 27 boxes. Each box contains a number, and if you add each row and column across and *through* the cube, and the diagonal lines through the centre of the cube, it comes to the same total.

Here is a magic cube which has been taken apart, and with only some of the numbers filled in. It is up to you to fill in the rest so that the total comes out the same every which way.

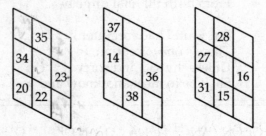

Answer 78

Q19. Nesting spheres

At a slum school in the twenties I was a hated 'clever dick', chased home almost daily by catcalling Cockney lads. But I toadied up to a strong boy known as 'Masher', and the bullying stopped. Under the protection of my minder I began to be a marbles capitalist.

The game was this. One boy would erect a 'castle' of three marbles against the playground wall. From a distance marked by a cloth cap, any boy could flip marbles and try to knock the castle down and claim the marbles. Marbles that missed were claimed by the owner of the 'pitch'.

I soon saw that the pitch owners did well and I found marble-poor boys in whom I invested the enormous capital of a few marbles to run a pitch for me. They got half the profit. I was soon a marbles tycoon with stacks of them.

I wanted to erect four marbles in a castle, and went to my engineer father about how to do it. 'It cannot be done. Only three spheres will 'nest' with each touching the other two,' he ordained. I accepted that then, but later I realised that my father had been wrong.

How can you nest more than three spheres, each touching all the others?

Answer 89

S   OF ON AN HA FA O   NOF H O H R

51

Q20. Unfair square

Professor Kalkalus wanted to humble Lady Pamela because she was so absurdly quick at arithmetic. She could make up magic squares while she was listening to the radio, chatting, reading a book and knitting. He worked out a tough problem, trying to trap her into a false assumption.

12	?	?	9
1	6	7	4
5	2	3	8
?	11	10	?

He showed her this incomplete magic square and challenged her to complete it. However, he added a difficult condition – integers between 3 and 12 were not allowed.

After a glance she said 'Silly man! You want me to pore over it for hours when you know very well it cannot be done. I shall not waste my time.'

'It is slightly unusual, but it can be solved by any computer and most competent mathematicians.'

'Pooh! Fiddlesticks!'

'It can be done. You will be furious if I can show you how, when you have sworn that it cannot. I know you are forced to try.'

'I'm a fool. It's absurd, but I'll give it an hour.'

She was back within the hour with the square filled in and complaining 'Cheat!'

What was her solution?

Answer 2

Q21. Never take the last

Once upon a time there were, in all social classes, what we then called 'manners' – by which we meant good deportment, the observance of certain accepted social behaviour customs. 'Manners ' varied with class, but most of them were sensible. Some were silly.

One silly one was that when a hostess offered, say, cakes from a plate, you should never take the last. If fully observed, this requirement must be wasteful. But guests would often say that they were full and could not eat a mite more, whilst greedily eying the last chocolate in the box or the last cake on the plate. They would never take the last one.

Now I was a visibly and hatefully clever little boy, and my equally clever Uncle Sydney decided to teach me humility. I managed to beat him at chess one day, so he changed the game and repeatedly beat me at a very simple game called 'Never Take The Last'. It was a game at which, he claimed, no one could ever beat him, even though he gave them every advantage.

To play the game you need forty or so counters, marbles, coins, dried peas or beans, matchsticks or whatever. My uncle produced a bag of farthings, and asked me to divide them into three piles, however I chose. He then gave me the choice of going first or second. Each of us in turn had to remove as many farthings as we wished from one (but only one) of the piles, even the whole pile if we so desired. The object was to force the other player to take the last farthing.

Monotonously my uncle won every time in scores of games, but I was learning. Through practice on my own at home and in many subsequent games with friends and relatives I learned how to be a tedious, repetitive winner.

Work out, as I did, the rules to ensure that you win every time.

Answer 21

SIX OF ONE AND HALF A DOZEN OF THE OTHER

Q22. Label correction

Caroline Penser was working out her notice after her alleged 'slipshod' weighing. Mr Poker sent her to the despatch room for the very humble task of receiving and delivering boxes of stores.

Three boxes came in from Department A with a note saying that all three were wrongly labelled because of sabotage by a man who had been dismissed. Luckily he had boasted to another worker, who told Mr Poker. One was labelled 'grotchets', another 'mongles', and the third 'mongles and grotchets'.

'Open them up, Caroline,' instructed Mr Poker, 'and find out what they are. Then correct the labels, all three of which are wrong. The boxes have to be closed and sealed as though they had never been opened, otherwise there will be complaints from the customers. So be careful, just take out as few items as possible from each box, and then carefully replace them, close each box, reseal it and label it correctly.'

Caroline relabelled the boxes and when Mr Poker came to inspect them he was pleased at first. 'I can't see where you have opened these two,' he said, 'and I can hardly see where this one was opened.'

Foolishly, Caroline said, 'But I only had to open one, of course.'

Mr Poker was even more pleased. There had been criticism from Personnel when he sacked Caroline. Now her unsuitability was quite clear.

'Just open *all* the boxes, Caroline, while I watch you. We must have this right. Guessing is simply no good.'

'But I wasn't guessing. As soon as I saw what was in this box I knew what must be in the others.'

'We do not rely on psychic powers, just get on with it.'

Caroline got on with it, and the boxes proved to be labelled correctly.

How did she do it?

Answer 32

Q23. Battle of the series

Lady Pamela felt that she had discovered a simple series that would defeat Professor Kalkalus. She wrote it down thus:

'0, 2, 6, 12, 20, ?, ?, 56'

She gave the professor ten minutes to correctly replace the question marks, but he gave the right answer after only five.

'How loathsomely clever you are, Corny,' she said. 'No wonder we all dislike you so much.'

'Come, Pam,' he replied, 'if I had failed you would have gloated for days, now wouldn't you?'

'How mean! You know what pleasure I get from gloating. To be a disgracefully slick mathematician is bad enough, but to deny a woman the chance to gloat is unforgivable. Go away!'

'To please you, anything, my dear. But first see if you can solve this. He wrote on a card the following incomplete series:

'0, 1, 4, 18, 100, ?, ?, 2028'

'I'll give you a day.'

'Do kindly be a pet and get lost when I ask. Pretty please, Corny dear,' said Lady Pamela.

'I go,' said Corny, 'I go. Look how I go; swifter than the arrow from a Tartar's bow*.' He lit one of the herbal cigarettes which she hated and turned back to his work.

Lady Pamela swept out, and came back in triumph within two hours with a pretty new dress and the answer.

'Tricky, Corny, but not tricky enough. Gloat, gloat. Ha, ha!'

What were the missing numbers and what was the principle in each case?

Answer 43

* From 'A Midsummer Night's Dream' - William Shakespeare

T E E'   E   T   ET   T   'T EE

Q24. Dividing land for heirs

In the middle of his large farm Farmer Bucol fenced off a plot of land consisting of five smaller plots for kitchen gardens, divided by hedges as shown below.

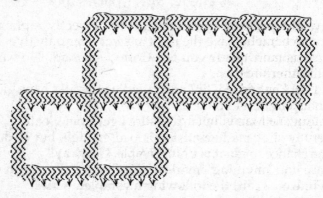

Each of these plots was allotted to one of his five grandchildren in his will, with the rest of the farm going to his son. But his youngest grandson, Herbert, moved in with him and his wife and helped them in their old age. Frederick, however, one of the other four grandchildren, left the land, moved to the city, and was cut out of the will.

Farmer Bucol's new will increased the area of the kitchen garden by 20%, and directed that half of the area belong to Herbert, and the other half be divided equally between the other three grandchildren.

However, as an ardent conservationist, he specified that only two of the sixteen hedges should be moved.

How was the additional area added and the whole redistributed having regard to these difficult conditions?

Answer 54

Q25. Throw out the gatecrasher

At a party beyond the grave a senior angel threw an intimate party to bring together those who had been in the same discipline on earth. Below is the list of those present. Which is the interloper?

Sir Humphrey Davey
Jons Jacob Berzelius
Hans Christian Ørsted
Ernest Rutherford
Linus Carl Pauling
Louis Pasteur
Pierre-Eugène Marcellin Berthelot

Answer 65

Q26. Powerful schoolboys

Tommy Butterworth and Teddy Johnson were fighting. They were in trouble enough without that. The new Headmaster at The Procrustes Secondary School believed passionately in Mixed Ability Classes. He had insisted on closing the Special Needs class and the clever children had been returned to work with the others as an improving influence and challenge. After a few disruptive days, the villains with surplus intelligence were excluded from the class – not to do advanced work, but on report for bad behaviour. This time they were to sit in the library with instructions to read a set book suitable for their age, and not to talk.

It was not a serious fight, just a scuffle to break the monotony. Tommy managed to twist Teddy's hand behind his back and

T E E'   O E OB   T O ET   T O 'T EE

boasted, with a mixture of styles: 'Victory to the strong! Concede defeat, wretched weakling, or I'll twist yer arm off.'

'Never! The Johnsons never surrender. Twist it off, you rotter!'

'Ouch! That really hurt, you clod.'

'Concede that I am the more powerful, and your suffering shall be relieved.'

'OK, fathead. You are more powerful.'

Once free, Teddy began to argue. 'An armlock proves nothing. A weak man can land one on a bouncer if he's nifty enough.'

'OK, but what is a test of power then?'

They were both mad on science and discussed a scientific test of power.

'Power is energy, isn't it? said Tommy. 'So how do you measure energy. What is the unit of measurement? Let's find out.'

After a look at Chambers Scientific, Teddy asked 'How many joules have you got, then?'

'More than you!'

'Prove it.'

Tommy went scrabbling through the library while Teddy did a crossword. 'I have it,' he exclaimed at the end of his research. Einstein showed that $E = Mc^2$. Energy is mass multiplied by the speed of light squared. Obviously the one with the most energy is the most powerful, and mass is the same as weight, so whichever of us is heavier is the more powerful. You weigh 45 kilograms, and I weigh 50 kilograms. So bow down and salute the most powerful boy in the room.'

'Speed of light squared. What nonsense! How can you square a speed? What is the square of 60 mph? I will accept that you are the stronger if you can tell me how many joules of energy you have and how many I have.'

They got interested in the problem, but it took a long time for them to get it right. Tommy got there first, using the Einstein equation above and two other equations which he discovered.

Force is measured in Newtons. One Newton (N) is the force required to accelerate 1 kilogram at 1 metre per second per second. Thus $N = kg \, m/s^2$.

Energy is measured in Joules (J). One joule is the energy required to exert a force of 1 Newton over 1 metre. Thus energy in joules is given by J = Nm.

A good enough approximation for c, the speed of light, is 300 million metres per second. Thus $c = 3 \times 10^8$ m/s.

How many joules of energy was available from the mass of each child?

Answer 76

Q27. Pamela's revenge

Lady Pamela Swot rang Professor Cornelius Kalkalus and invited him to a foxhunt.

'You invite me to join the unspeakable in pursuit of the uneatable? That is hardly a favour.'

'That wretched tag from Convict Wilde. He was none too speakable himself, to judge by the contemporary view.'

'I cannot see what pleasure you get from running down either a very great dead writer, who was torn to pieces by his critics and the law, or a beautiful live creature, that will run until it drops from exhaustion and is torn to pieces by slavering hounds. Further, I cannot see why you should want to inflict such a heartless spectacle on me.'

'Corny dear, I want to free you from corroding cant. We belong to a species that survived only as a hunter for the first million years of its existence. We have learned to live as agriculturalists for a few thousand. We should not have survived unless we had an instinctive love of the chase. You spend hours watching murderous TV chases by humans with human prey. You have the instinct for the chase as we all do. The hullabaloo about hunting is a crank new idea a decade or two old. It will fade. I am certain

T E E' NONE O B N A T O E T AT ON'T EE

you will surprise yourself at the pleasure you get.'

'Forget it, Pamela.'

'All right, but I have a problem for you. I have a four by four magic square. I shall fill in half the numbers in their proper place, and I bet you cannot solve it.'

'Come on, Pamela. Those things take me two minutes.'

'I bet! Suggest stakes.'

'All right, my girl. If I solve it, you never go hunting again. If I fail, I accept your invitation to the hunt.'

'A bit uneven. You endure one hunt, but I lose a beloved hobby.'

'OK. You give up for a season, or I go whenever you invite me for a season.'

'Done! I'll send you the incomplete magic square. But there is one condition. I specify the highest number you may use.'

This is the square that she sent him, and her rule was that no number on the square shall be higher than 8.

Can you solve it?

Answer 87

8		1	
	5		4
	3		6
2		7	

Q28. Squaring the pyramid

In the Special Needs room Tommy was messing about with plasticine while Teddy was boning up on regular solids: cubes, cylinders, polyhedra and so on. He was using an A-level primer which he should not have had a glimpse at for five years yet.

Seeing Teddy so deeply absorbed, Tommy used an elastic band between his fingers as a catapult to flick a fold of paper covered with honey, from their secret jar, at his companion's neck where it stuck in his hair. The resulting pelting contest lasted twelve minutes and ended in a scuffle on the floor.

'Uncivilised brute,' said Teddy.

'Rotter,' responded Tommy.

Hearing footsteps, they scrambled up and resumed the appearance of study. Their teacher, Mr Dominie, appeared at the door to see how they were getting on. The debris of their pelting match was clearly visible, but fortunately he was preoccupied.

'Do you need anything?' he asked.

No answer.

'Have you any questions?'

Tommy had one. 'Whichever way I cut a sphere, like an orange, the cut surface is a circle. Is a sphere the only form like that?' Mr Dominie thought for a moment. 'A cube,' he said. 'Whichever way you cut it you get a square.'

Tommy thought 'Rubbish!' but said 'Oh yes, thank you Sir.'

After the teacher had gone, Teddy said 'He's not right, is he?'

'Check up for yourself with your plasticine,' answered Tommy.

They made a cube out of plasticine and tried to cut it various ways, but cutting deformed it so they began again with an apple which Teddy had with him. They cut a cube from it, and soon found that they could generate triangles, rectangles and other quadrilaterals by a single plane cut.

Then Teddy used his apple to make a regular tetrahedron – a pyramid with four equal faces, each an equilateral triangle.

He challenged Tommy to make a single plane cut to produce an exact square face.

Tommy swore it could not be done, and was ready to bet twenty marbles on it. Teddy attempted a demonstration. Had he lost his marbles?

Answer 98

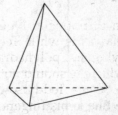

Q29. Reading impossible drawings

Caroline started work in the design office. There were many drawing boards and computers with indolent workers, mostly men, smoking and chatting, and occasionally drawing a line on a board.

She was set to work out the principles of the draughtsman's art under a supercilious young apprentice called Billy Brain who showed her what a front elevation, side elevation and a plan were. Then, having heard of her reputation for cleverness, he decided to humble her.

He gave her a few sets of drawings, each consisting of a plan and two elevations, and asked her to do a 3D sketch of each object. She quickly and easily solved most of them, but was worried about one which Billy had put in as a trick question, knowing that the three drawings were mutually inconsistent.

'You'll never be a draughtsman,' he taunted, as she studied the drawings carefully. 'Surely you can see what that is!'

'I know what it is, Mr Brain, but I am wondering how I could possibly draw it.'

'You have fallen into my trap,' laughed Billy. 'Anyone with a grain of sense could see that there is no such object.'

'There is you know, Mr Brain,' she said.

He laughed again, and went away telling the tale all round the office.

This is what Caroline was faced with.

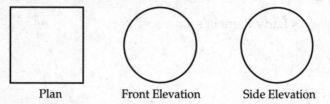

| Plan | Front Elevation | Side Elevation |

She kept at it, and later she produced a drawing and a description of the object. Had she got a solution? Is there an object which matches these drawings, and if so, whatever is it?

Answer 19

Q30. Multiplying magic squares

Professor Kalkalus took it ill that he had been beaten on a magic square. He rang Lady Pamela and asked her out to dinner. She met him at the Athenaeum with a sable wrap over a flowered dress, that together must have cost her a fortune.

'You look like a cross between a rich whore and a fashion model who borrows the stock. But under the paint you are lovely.'

Corny was in a dinner jacket over grey flannels, and sported a green, ill-tied, bow tie. He wore muddy trainers. Lady Pamela had to redo his bow tie before they would let him in.

'You look like a mathematics professor who has been given the part of a cardboard city tramp in the school play,' she complained. 'I know you do it on purpose. Your nails are dirty, but your beard looks nice.'

Over the calves' liver and Volnay he disclosed the puzzle.

'Take the powers of two up to the eighth – 2, 4, 8 etc – and make a three by three magic square where the *product*, not the sum, of all rows and diagonals is a constant. You have a week.

'It is impossible. I shall not try.'

'You know you will.'

She solved it three weeks later. She put the answer in a letter which she dated for the day after the dinner. She put it in a used envelope with an appropriate date stamp, and sent her chauffeur round to deliver it surreptitiously – faking a late delivery.

Neither referred to the matter for some time.

What was Lady Pamela's solution?

Answer 3

THERE'S NONE SO BLIND AS THOSE THAT WON'T SEE

Q31. Ermyntrude and the law

This introduces Ermyntrude. This lightish verse, exposing her vices, has been stripped of the triple rhymes which it features. They are listed in random order at the end of the de-rhymed verse.

If you want to benefit from the warning of her unhappy story, you will have to fit them back where they belong.

But can you do it? I beg leave to doubt it.

Ermyntrude and the law

The trouble with young
Was not that she was rough or
The problem was her
The horrid, pert, presumptuous
Had got to be a horrid
And understand an awesome

What licence has a child of
To go beyond her
And read and write like you and
Her family life was just a
For what endears an infant
Than beating Dad and Mum at

Her poor young teacher was
When teaching her the
To find the little demon
To know Cyrillic, Roman,
And Hebrew too. Amazing
Even in such a forward

Is not advanced
Without due
Improper in a child of
Her worried Head at once
The infant had a Special
She felt compelled to act with

64

She sent for a
To test, assess and thus
With this scholastic
The Ed. Psych. tested her for
Many a time, in many
Until he fell into a

They found that she was testing
Resulting in the rather
Conclusion that the man was
They tried detention and the
And other punishments, in
It only sharpened up her

They put her under freezing
They talked to her for hours and
And even gave her sweets and
But could not make her
So now by Law throughout the
All such Precocity is

These are the rhymes that have been stripped away. Can you replace them? Within twenty minutes?

Ermyntrude Banned hours dim flowers cane speed Need rude tot three grim anarchist understand attitude ABC vain showers Land him brain psychologist me ways agreed swot alphabet assist seniority days Greek mess lot chess freak daze orthography cheek less three upset get

Answer 31

Q32. The A-Z of X-words

For the thousandth time that day, the Quick Brown Fox jumped over the Lazy Dog. The dog, too idle to get up, merely growled.
   'Why are you always doing that?' asked the dog.

'There are only twenty-six letters in the English alphabet,' barked the fox, 'and my jumps indicate the shortest English sentence any one has found which contains all twenty-six letters. The sentence fits them into a mere thirty-three letters.'

'I am always being insulted as lazy,' whined the dog, 'and you are complimented on your speed. This is species-ist discrimination of the worst sort.'

'What can you do about it? You'll never find a shorter sentence with all the letters in it.'

The Lazy Dog pulled itself together, gritted its teeth, summoned up all its resolution . . . . and got up.

'I cannot compose a shorter sentence, but I will compose a crossword puzzle that uses all the letters of the alphabet once and no more.'

'Bet you can't! To start with you'll never finish it or, at the finish, you'll never start.'

'I take your bet. I will compose it and put five of the letters in position for you. The bet is this. If I do it and you solve it, I owe you ten bones. If you fail, then you promise never to jump over me again.'

'And deprive a million typists?'

'You are on. What do I care?'

It took the Lazy Dog days. Lassitude nearly won, but in the end this was displayed on the screen of his computer.

Quick as he was, the Brown Fox failed to solve it, causing consternation in a thousand typing pools.

Can you do better?

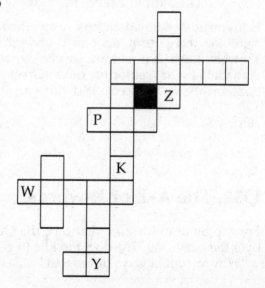

Answer 42

Q33. A problem with a virus

Caroline Penser was doing rather too well on the drawing office PC. Mr Jimmy Hacker, who was supposed to be instructing her, was irritated by her facile learning and eagerness to get her hands on it. There was too little awed attention, and too much 'I think I have it, Mr Hacker; I can manage now'.

So he set her a trap. He knew a little virus, and gave her a job to do on a disc that he had infected. She worked for a time, and then called up an addition that appeared on the screen like this:

```
        (   %   ,   $
        )   &   -   %
        *   '   $   &
        +   (   %   '
        ,   )   &   (
        -   *   '   )
        ─────────────
        (   %   '   (   )
```

After watching in the background, Hacker came back. 'Oh dear, those figures are vital,' he said. 'Your work is satisfactory, Caroline, but you are getting overconfident. We shall have to see if we can get you out of this dreadful mess you have muddled yourself into.'

'I think I'd learn better if you let me work it out myself, Sir.'

'Overconfident again. Well, just to teach you a lesson, I will tolerate the waste of time. If you have not solved it in an hour I hope you will agree when you need help in the future.'

Caroline got into the program controlling the display and noticed that the ASCII* code for the wrong symbols increased by one in each column as she went down, except in one case.

* American Standard Code for Information Interchange

D   E D E D E E   E

She figured that the true digits obeyed the same rule, and that they also increased by one as you descend each column. She soon worked out the only arrangement that gave the right total.

When Hacker returned she was far ahead with another task. He shook his finger at her. 'Aha! Given up, I see. Now I do hope you will be a little less sure of yourself in future.'

'Sorry, Sir. I should have waited. I finished the sum some time ago but you were busy and rather than waste time I got on with something else. Here it is, Sir.'

She pressed a key and the calculation appeared on the screen in the correct format, with the answer displayed.

What was the answer, and can you complete the rest of the calculation?

Much more difficult, and for the computerate only, what was the computer error induced by the virus?

Answer 53

Q34. Every which way

Since people first made signs to represent meaning on leather, clay, papyrus, bricks and what have you, there have been different methods of sequencing the symbols. Vertical up, vertical down, horizontal left to right and right to left. They have even used both together – backwards and forwards, left then right then left again like ploughing.

Which makes sense. Think of all the energy wasted on carriage returns by typists and by people switching their eyes back across a page to start a new line when reading. A ploughman would think you were daft if you suggested doing a wasted journey across the field to start each fresh furrow.

I have been lucky enough in the course of sixty years of holiday and business travel to see a lot of the world. But, devious as I am, I am incapable of making a straightforward list. In the display below I have secreted some of the cities I have visited. My sequencing goes, like the map scribbles of my wanderings, any which way – starting anywhere, finishing anywhere, striking in any direction, but always travelling in a straight line.

There are, in the grid, twenty well known world cities. But they want to regain their unique, special, national and local character. They can only do so if someone sorts them out and re-establishes their identity.

Are you equal to this mammoth task?

V	E	I	K	E	Y	O	R	I	A	C
A	N	P	C	A	M	C	Y	V	U	A
O	D	I	B	U	A	A	I	N	R	O
E	N	M	F	R	L	V	D	A	Y	B
S	O	A	D	F	A	M	K	R	N	K
B	E	I	P	L	G	N	I	N	I	G
O	F	A	E	L	A	F	O	L	R	D
F	W	T	T	F	E	B	C	O	A	A
O	Y	K	O	T	S	S	M	S	K	N
C	N	A	M	I	L	E	R	H	U	S
H	U	L	L	A	P	E	R	T	H	K

Answer 64

D   N   N   E D E D   EN E   E

Q35. Catching Caroline

Catching Caroline Penser began to be an obsession in the drawing office at Meredith's. She was becoming a competent draughtsman, so three of the juniors got into a huddle to humble her. They prepared the two views below.

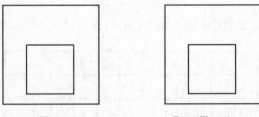

Plan   Front Elevation

They persuaded her immediate supervisor to join the plot, so he dropped by her desk saying, 'Just add an isometric projection to this drawing so that the workmen can visualise the part better.'

Caroline looked at the drawing doubtfully. It did not look genuine. She looked up at him. 'An isometric projection of this? Whatever is it for?'

'I suppose you don't know what an isometric is.'

'A 3D view; but what is this part for, and what is the order number?'

'Never you mind! Just do it. I'll add the details later. Why do you always argue instead of doing as you are told?'

'I like to understand.'

'You are only sixteen.'

'That is why.'

He returned after an hour to hear her confession of failure. 'Well?' he asked.

'Well what?'

'The isometric.'

'Oh. That! I didn't think you could be serious.

'You can't do it, can you?'

'I can do it, but it makes no sense.'

'Admit it! You can't do it.'

'Let me look at it again. Yes, there are two answers.' She paused and drew on a scribble pad. 'There you are. It could be like this, or this. But what could be the use of it?'

Is there an object that fits the specification? What were her two drawings like?

Answer 75

Q36. Metamorphosis

Some animals change forms and life-styles to subsist at different sizes and different stages in their life. For example, egg, caterpillar, chrysalis, beetle. They are subject to metamorphosis.

The seven creatures listed opposite also have larger and quite different forms. If you are very clever and can find the right three letters to add at either end, you can create seven 9-letter English words.

Answer 86

1.   ... A P E ...

2.   ... R A T ...

3.   ... C A T ...

4.   ... A N T ...

5.   ... C U R ...

6.   ... H E N ...

7.   ... E W E ...

DO N MON   E DE D MEN E   M E

71

Q37. Keeping Ermyntrude occupied

Fairly literate and numerate at four and a half, Ermyntrude was hard to handle in a mixed ability class where the slow ones absorbed so much of the teacher's time. Mrs Teresa Char liked Ermyntrude but it was hard work to keep her interested and away from day-dreaming.

Ermyntrude loved puzzles and had just discovered and begun to delight in word squares. Mrs Char photocopied one from a book and told one of the girls carefully to white out all but a few of the letters. Then she gave it to Ermyntrude to solve.

'Fill in the square,' she said, 'to show six 6-letter words, the same down as across.

Ermyntrude struggled for half an hour, writing and rubbing out, and then began to look unhappy. 'I can't do it,' she said. 'It's too hard.' She fell to day-dreaming.

As soon as she found time Mrs Char came to help. 'Oh dear! I forgot to give you the letters. It will be easier if I give you the rest of the letters and then all you have to do is fit them into the square. I'm sure you can do it now.'

These are the letters which Mrs Char wrote down:

C E E E E E E E E E I I L L M M N N O O R R R S S S S T T

But overchallenged, and having begun an attractive, creative day-dream, Ermyntrude took no further interest in the problem. She failed, but she was only four and a half.

How old are you? Can you do it?

Answer 97

Q38. Goldilocks Ermyntrude

During lunch Mrs Char thought of a puzzle for Ermyntrude, who was a small girl for her age but pretty with bright yellow, curly hair. She scrambled the words of a song about Goldilocks, intending to set Ermyntrude to work out the verse from the words.

After lunch she said to Ermyntrude, 'This is just for you. It is a song about a girl with very yellow hair called Goldilocks. I will give you the words all mixed up. You see if you can put them together properly. Then I might teach you the tune.'

She gave the child this, written on a piece of paper.

STRAWBERRIES NOT DISHES SEW SWINE CUSHION BE GOLDILOCKS MINE A SEAM NOR SUGAR FEED FEED FINE GOLDILOCKS SHALT THOU WASH UPON CREAM WILT THOU YET AND THE AND A AND BUT ON SIT

Answer 18

Q39. Ermyntrude squares accounts

A few days later Ermyntrude brought Mrs Char an incomplete solution of the word square she had failed to solve. She was miffed by her failure, and asked for another one to try. Mrs Char was busy but she persuaded a senior prefect to find a word square and white out most of the letters, and then list the missing letters at the bottom.

She gave it to Ermyntrude as homework. Ermyntrude solved it using her computer and only the tiniest help from her mother and the computer dictionary. She brought it in triumph to Mrs Char next day, full of herself. 'There you are, see! See! I can do them!'

DO N AMON   E DEAD MEN LE   M L E

Mrs Char sighed. 'You are clever, Ermyntrude, but you'll never be lovable.'

Can you do as well as Ermyntrude? Here is the square. The missing letters are:

A A A A E E E E I I
M M N N N R R T T

Answer 29

L				S
		N		
S				S

Q40. Wriggle reading

Here is a can of worms in the form of a grid of jumbled letters which seem to make no sense at all. Beneath this chaos lies order if you can but find it.

If they start always from the central M, clever word-masters will be able to find as many as eight 11-letter words in wriggling worm spelling, radiating out from the central M, reading any way.

Warning! Mark the letters as you use them. They may not be used twice.

I	N	G	Y	M	A	N	G	W
L	E	P	S	E	K	I	L	O
L	E	T	S	N	T	A	R	R
U	L	A	I	O	E	L	E	K
C	R	T	A	M	A	E	D	I
I	C	R	A	O	E	O	T	C
S	H	E	E	U	L	I	N	H
S	I	R	N	N	A	N	C	O
E	N	O	I	A	T	C	I	L

Answer 4

Q41. Crossword for the clueless

Crossword buffs are spoiled. They are given clues, be they plain or cryptic. I am against this soft policy and stand out for rigour.

This crossword puzzle is partly filled in and you, utterly clueless, have to complete it. To make things harder, there is a restriction. You may not choose from the alphabet in the usual way. You may use each letter only once, which means you must use each letter as there are only 26 empty spaces.

A B C D E F G H I J K L M
N O P Q R S T U V W X Y Z

Answer 41

DOWN AMONG THE DEAD MEN LET HIM LIE

Q42. Another scrambled aphorism

I am a shamelessly immodest, clever old devil – probably the cleverest in the world. For instance, I had this appointment for a repair to my muddy, battered old Volvo but when I got to the garage they had been delayed on a job and could not do the repair. Having expressed my annoyance I did not drive home, but sought to make the best of things.

I sought advantage from my setback. To save a wasted journey I decided on a much needed car wash. I drove into the auto-wash, put into the slot my token for the most elaborate wash programme. Now before I proceed I want you to remember that I am possibly the most intelligent person in the world. Bear that in mind as I tell you the fault in the car that I wanted fixed.

The driver's side window was stuck in the down position! I could not get it up.

Once you are in a car wash with the trundling sprayer and scrubber passing, you cannot get out.

The first pass of the machine was a light rinse. My face and clothing were soaked, and the sharp spray stung. I got cold. The hot rinse was painful, but at least stopped the shivering. It was the heavy wash cycle with squirting suds and the enormous revolving scrubbing brushes that was most troublesome. People have noticed that the right side of my face is rather cleaner than the left since that day. Then came the long freezing rinse. The dogged old Volvo was soon up to my knees with swilling filthy suds.

I drove home, my feet awash, soaked to the skin – but half clean, mind you, clean on the one side, sad and wiser.

All this may give you a clue to knit up this unravelled aphorism which I wrote as soon as I was dry. I have cut most of the words in half and mixed them up.

AGA LIGENCE STUP NO INST HI IS INTEL DEF GH IDITY ENCE

Can you repair my damage and rebuild my aphorism?

Answer 52

Q43. Sort this lot out

The only clue to this I can give is that more recently educated solvers may be handicapped. Serve them right!

Here are a number of words. They differ in many ways, but in one way they fall into two simple classes, three words in each.

Classify them and explain the difference between the two classes.

> imitate aphorism monkey try idea speculate

Answer 63

Q44. Seeking connections

Find the word which is the thought-link between: an experienced seaman, a popular name for the flag of a great nation, the unwanted burden of a sailor from Asia Minor, and a circle song to greet a new beginning

Answer 74

Q45. Listing deprived lists

Ermyntrude fell in love with a Thesaurus when she found one in the school library, to which she had been sent because she was so far ahead of the class, bored and disruptive. The Head was passing the library, looked in and saw that Ermyntrude had

A B D	A D	B

written on the blackboard as follows:

1	.	*a*	.	*a*	.	*o*	.	*u*	.
2	.	*n*	.	*e*	.	*t*	.	*r*	.
3	.	*h*	.	*s*	.	*u*	.	*u*	.
4	.	*r*	.	*g*	.	*a*	.	*m*	.
5	.	*l*	.	*a*	.	*a*	.		
6	.	*i*	.	*t*	.	*o*	.	*a*	. *y*
7	.	*l*	.	*s*	.	*a*	.	*y*	
8	.	*e*	.	*i*	.	*o*	.		
9	.	*a*	.	*e*	.	*t*	.	*e*	.
10	.	*o*	.	*t*	.	*r*			
11	.	*c*	.	*e*	.	*u*	.	*e*	
12	.	*e*	.	*i*	.	*t*	.	*r*	

'Now Ermyntrude,' said the Head, 'you are making a good try. The letters are well formed, but what you have written makes no sense. Also, you use a full stop only at the end of a sentence. Now tell me dear, what are you trying to write?'

'It's not a try, Miss. It's what I wanted to write.'

'But no-one could read it, Ermyntrude. It is nonsense.'

'I think you could read the words if I told you something that would help you.'

'What nonsense, child. Whatever are you talking about?'

'It's a sort of hard-to-read writing I made up for fun, leaving out some of the letters. It's a sort of list of lists.'

The Head said, quite kindly, 'I'm afraid you are wasting your time, dear. We must have *structure*.' She found a primer and set the child to read simple sentences, which she did . . . until the Head left the room.

What was Ermyntrude up to? What can *you* make of it all?

Answer 85

78

Q46. The one that is left behind

At Anton's, Lady Pamela finished her caviar and said, 'I prefer Beluga.'

Professor Kalkalus said nothing. He spread another slice, added lemon and ate it between sips of vodka.

After the Crêpes Suzettes ceremony, with all the flamboyance and flame, she said nothing but ate nothing. He knew something was brewing.

'Come Pam,' he said, 'what are you cooking up. You are in your mischievous mood.'

'I hate being called Pam. I shall punish you with a simple mathematical matchstick trick which you will dismally fail to solve. This will infuriate you.'

'Is there a bet on this?'

'Another day with the hounds, against . . .'

'Against what, my dear?'

'My All, my love.'

'On!' urged the Professor.

'Remember, you will be furious and you will fail. If not both, you win.'

The waiter was summoned and having offered a lighter, unhappily brought a plebian box of matches and a garish large ashtray. Smoking was discouraged at Anton's.

Lady Pamela laid out the matches thus:

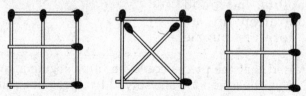

'It's simple and straightforward,' she said. 'There can be no wriggling, no bending or breaking. You can do it or you cannot. I

A B D   H HA D   H   H B H

have placed eighteen matches on the table. You are to take away seven, no more, and leave behind on the table just one.

'Like all the best puzzles, it appears impossible.'

The Professor studied the matches for ten minutes and then said, 'As I feared. It is not a good puzzle but merely a silly joke. It not only looks it but it really is impossible. I thought the bet was too rash to be true. What a nasty little tease you are!'

'You give up to easily,' retorted Lady Pamela. 'I am sad. It shows how little you value my poor little All.'

Was she a wicked tease, or is there a valid answer? Might she have to surrender her All?

Answer 96

Q47. Kid fits bits

Ermyntrude at the age of four was not allowed scissors. Left to study alone because of her precocious surplus ability, she found this illustration in an ancient, foreign puzzle book.

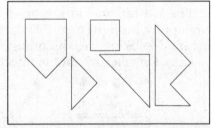

She guessed that the pieces could be fitted together to make a square. During the afternoon she solved two problems: she found a way to fit them together without copying or cutting the paper, or changing it in any way. And she showed the correctly assembled square. No-one ever knew she had done it, or how. Until now.

Can you equal the infant's achievements under the same constraints?

Answer 17

Q48. Leaving things

If you cannot solve this then you should give up puzzling.

Rahman Abdulla was old and had gold, much gold. He wanted to leave his gold to one of his three sons rather than divide it and diminish the hoard. More than that, feeble and lonely, he wanted the love, respect and attention of his beloved sons, despite the fact that they – with businesses to run, several wives each and enormous families – could spare him very little time.

Trying to be reasonable, Rahman Abdulla made a will leaving everything to the son that came closest to meeting the following condition. 'Allah alone knows how many days I have left to live,' he said. The son whose number of visits to me shall be a third of the number of days that I live shall inherit.' And it was so written.

Although no-one knew how long he would live, when the old man went to his rest one son had made exactly the right number of visits. The others were wildly out. How did Farouk, the clever one, manage it?

This is a Kickself problem. You will kick yourself if you fail.

Answer 28

Q49. Odd one out

The aliens from outer space have yet another test. Your must find the impostor, the odd-one-out, in this list of integers:

    7,245 8,991 1,548 1,233 8,127 6,354 5,645 6,633

You must find it quickly or you die. YOU HAVE TWO MINUTES.

Answer 39

```
    A B RD    H HA D SW R H W    H B SH
```

Q50. Monochrome wires

When I was young – a long time ago – I was a wood machinist and I worked in a very primitive factory which would have been the delight of a modern industrial archaeologist. The machinery was mounted on heavy wooden flooring under which, in a hideous dark cavern, there was an enormous electric motor which looked as if had been designed by Faraday himself.

The stator was a great U-magnet of cast iron and the commutator flashed blue sparks the whole time, making the otherwise unlit subterranean zone a place of wonder and terror with a great array of long spindles with many diameters of pulleys, and unprotected leather belts which came up through the floor to drive our machines.

We machinists had to be our own millwrights. We had to know how to repair everything, to oil or scrape a bronze bearing which was heating up, mend the heavy leather belts – and worry out the electrical problems when the one great motor failed.

In the middle of a wet and windy night-shift the motor gave out and I, as 'the clever one', had to sort out the electric so-called system that Brunel would have called outdated. In the early days of electricity there was insulated wire. The idea of multi-coloured wires had not occurred to anyone. Some wires had blown and I needed to use three spare wires. Three identical brown wires, with one end of each by the motor and the other under a manhole about half a mile away at the other end of the factory site. I needed to label both ends of each wire correctly. I had my bicycle battery and bulb so I could test for continuity.

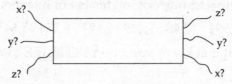

How did I correctly label the six ends with no more than one journey across the pitch-black factory site in the cold and rain?

Answer 5

Q51. How much wood in a log?

Those who dealt in wood in England in the past seem to have had little to do with mathematicians. When I joined the trade, I smelled a rat when I learned the normal way of calculating the volume of wood in a log.

'Measure the length to the nearest foot,' said my mentor. I measured it with a tape as 14 feet. 'Then you will want to know the average area,' he continued. 'The log tapers, so take the middle. Use this tape to measure the girth – just wrap it round the log.'

The tape was a 'quarter girth tape'; its 'inches' were each four inches long. The log was on battens, and passing the tape round it I was able to measure a number, which was a quarter of the circumference in inches. The log measured 26 of these 'inches'.

'What do I do now?' I asked.

'Ah! That's the tricky bit. You have to multiply the quarter-girth by itself and then multiply that by the length in feet, and finally divide by 144. Don't ask me why, that's what we always have to do.'

'What does that give you?' I asked humbly. I was a learner of twenty-odd.

'That gives you the cubic feet in the log.'

'It can't,' I foolishly cried.

'Oh yes it can! That's the way we've done it from way back. It was a chap called Hoppus who corrected the bad old ways of measuring wood in the seventeenth century. We call it a Hoppus measure. Don't worry about it, it's hard to pick up at first.'

Then he showed me the Hoppus or quarter-girth tables which did the multiplying for you. You read the length against the quarter-girth and there was the answer in so-called cubic feet. I checked the arithmetic of the table and found his astonishing formula was confirmed. I was appalled. The diameter of a log was being calculated as circumference divided by four. The whole of the world trade in logs was based on an error – the hypothesis that $\pi = 4$. It still is, as far as I know.

A B RD N H HAND S W R H W N H B SH

I have two problems for you. First, the easy one. Assuming the log were a cylinder, what was the true volume of a Hoppus cubic foot and how many true cubic feet were there in my log?

Now for the hard one. Knowing that, on average a log is best represented as a truncated cone, what was the second error of the Hoppus method, and how could we more accurately estimate the volume of wood in a log?

Answer 51

Q52. Can they be random?

Randomness is a tricky concept. The usual definition of a random series of numbers is one where no selection from the series is predictive of, or influences, any other section.

Here are a number of series. Which of them are, and which of them cannot be, random series?

1, 2, 3, 4, 5, 6, 7, 8

1, 2, 3, 5, 7, 11, 13, 17

21, 675, 0, 23498, 6, 43

2, 4, 8, 16, 32, 64, 128

9, 3, 273, 12, 22234, -73, 201

3, 9, 27, 81, 243

Answer 62

Q53. Teddy's funny tots

Tommy was scribbling down some sums, while Teddy read a book about Clark Maxwell.

Here are Teddy's sums:

$$1 + 3 = 7$$
$$2 = 3 = 5$$
$$0 + 1 = 8$$
$$7 + 3 = 8$$
$$6 = 6$$
$$7 = 3$$

He showed them to Tommy who said, 'All wrong! I always said your arithmetic pongs.'

'You pong, and so do your whole family. Well, except your sister Sue. If you were not so deeply dim you would see that my sums are right 'in the right context', as Mr Dominie would say.

'Hello, what's this we hear? Sue! Who's sweet on Sue? A grubby little monkey like you? She'd never look at you!'

Teddy blushed, looked bashful, and returned to his arithmetic.

'If those equations are true, then puzzle this out. What do these numbers equal? 1. 4. 9.'

Tommy thought for a while and then gave up. 'Bet you can't tell me and prove it,' he challenged.

'I'll bet. If I win you keep quiet to the boys about what I said about Sue.'

'I would never split to that lot anyway.'

'And Sue? Don't say a word?'

'If you win!'

What do the numbers 1, 4 and 9 equal?

Answer 73

A BIRD IN THE HAND IS WORTH TWO IN THE BUSH

Q54. A disagreeable word

Which of these words is disagreeable – the stranger in the grammatic camp?

CASH   HAMMER   MATE   RAGE   ROAST   TEACH   RUN

Answer 84

Q55. On the hunt for birds

In this beautiful lush, green, virgin rain-forest you are bird watching. But the birds are hiding artfully. They see your telescope. It is a gun to them, so they conceal themselves every which way they can. You will never find them all. Yet if you miss one, and fail to put it in your Yellow Birdwatcher's Book, how ashamed you will be in front of the others in the party.

Seventy of you flew in to the forest airstrip that morning from Miami on a 'Bargain Wild Watcher's Wonder Trip'. You are tripping over watchers everywhere you go. Don't let them see your book!

There are 21 birds to find. Such an odd variety too for a forest. A bit contrived?

You simply must record them all.

Answer 95

S	W	A	L	L	O	W	I	P	B
E	P	I	G	E	O	N	S	L	T
A	G	A	N	N	E	T	A	O	I
G	D	A	R	T	A	C	Y	V	T
U	O	U	I	R	K	R	A	E	E
L	D	K	L	B	O	O	J	R	V
L	O	I	I	K	O	W	L	K	O
L	N	R	T	H	R	U	S	H	D
G	D	T	N	A	S	A	E	H	P
R	E	H	S	I	F	G	N	I	K

Q56. Going straight for a long way

Any building trade worker knows this. But can you work it out as an original first principles problem? Be like the unknown genius who thought of it first. Builders may not answer.

If you need to draw a straight line to which to cut or paint, you can use a straight edge – a thin, flat, ground, steel bar up to two or even three metres long. But what if you want to make a very long dead straight line on a long wall, a road or a plank? It does not work to pace along with a straight edge – it never comes out really straight.

You could stretch a piece of string or cord but you cannot draw a line along it without moving it, and workmen don't carry theodolites. So what do you do, Mr Original Thinker?

Answer 16

Q57. Wonky wisdom

A wise phrase – an aphorism – has gone wonky. It has been mishandled and disturbed. Please, for the future of mankind, set it straight. Please, set it straight! Five minutes is par.

EVERY RIGHTS HIS ARE ACCORD EQUAL HIS SHOULD RESPONSIBILITIES CAPACITY BE IN WITH MAN'S BUT

Answer 27

G   A   G A   N

Q58. As ? is to ? so is ? to ?

A relationship is often as hard to see as a conflict is easy to see. Here we have a puzzle where you are shown a complex relationship between one set of entities and you have to apply it to another set so as to find the answer from a limited set of alternatives. There are only four options, so do not get too excited if you get it right. Twenty-five per cent of barbary apes or horses could do as well!

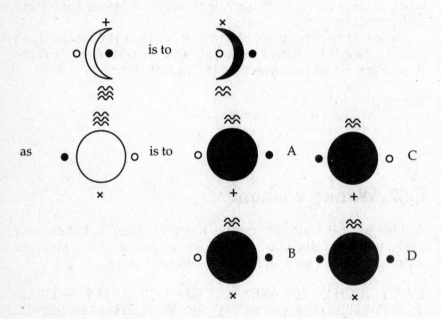

All you have to do is to decide which of the four alternatives has the same relationship with the set figure as that between the top pair.

Answer 38

Q59. General unwanted knowledge

I shall question you ruthlessly on the impedimenta of unnecessary knowledge that we all find burdening our brains – facts which can be looked up when needed and where there is no need to know, except for the very unusual purpose of answering General Knowledge quizzes.

1. From which author and play does the character Iago come?

2. What is the name of the inhabited island off Vancouver, Canada?

3. What is the chemical name for common salt?

4. Who was the American President who succeeded Nixon?

5. How many farthings were there in a 1920 pound sterling?

6. Which American city is called 'Mile High City'? In which state is it?

7. What was the name in British Imperial days of Sri Lanka, and what was its pre-Imperial name?

8. What is the capital of Tasmania and where is that country?

9. In the northern hemisphere the zero meridian passes through a museum and a park. Which museum and which park? Who owns the park?

10. Polished oak displays 'figure' – distinctive untextured streaks. What are they?

Answer 49

GO   A   U G A   OU   U   N

Q60. Mon conversion

'Quelle religion as-tu, Victor?' asked the French priest who took us for French and religious studies. He was testing my French, not conducting an inquisition.

I replied, 'Comme mon père, je suis atheist.'

Père Hubert replied calmly in English. 'Firstly I have to tell you that the French word for 'atheist' is 'athée'. Secondly I require you to leave this Christian company immediately and stand in the hall. You are not to return until you have become a Proper Christian Boy.'

I left. I stood in the hall. It was boring, but I stood by my priciples . . . . for seven minutes and twelve seconds. Then I knocked on the door.

'Entrez!'

I put my head round the door.

'Eh bien! Parles-tu?'

'Je suis un Proper Christian Boy, Monsieur.'

'Prends ta place, encore. Resume your place,' he said. Then loudly, turning to the class, 'Et continuons!'

The matter was closed. I was converted.

Now I have to set you a much more difficult conversion job. You have to take this matchstick design and by moving no more than four matches convert it to three triangles.

Hold! There is a further restriction – they have to be equilateral triangles. More! No match may be removed, only moved.

Answer 6

Q61. Einstein quotation

Albert Einstein used to tell this subtle tale which says a lot about human understanding.

Little Hans had been blind from birth, but was a bit of a wag. Albert was speaking to him, and mentioned a white flower.

Hans interrupted. 'What is 'white', Uncle Albert?'

Albert: 'It is the colour of a swan.'

Hans: 'So what is a swan, Uncle?'

Albert: 'It is a bird with a curved neck.'

Hans: 'But what is a curve?'

Albert: 'Ah! There I can help at last.' He took the child's hand and moved it in the form of a swan-neck curve. 'There! That is a curve.'

Hans (laughing): 'Ah! So now I know what 'white' means?'

Here is another scrambled aphorism from that great man. Can you sort it out and reassemble it? I have broken it into word-pairs as a rare indulgence, although there is one single word.

HAVE ALWAYS / AND FULFILS / PREJUDICES BUT /
GREAT SPIRITS / CLEAR FORM / THE DUTY / A MAN /
VIOLENT OPPOSITION / CANNOT UNDERSTAND / DOES NOT /
FROM MEDIOCRITIES / HIS INTELLIGENCE / TO EXPRESS /
THOUGHTLESSLY SUBMIT / THE RESULTS / THE LATTER /
OF HIS / COURAGEOUSLY USES / THOUGHTS IN / IT WHEN /
HONESTLY AND / TO HEREDITARY / FOUND

Answer 61

GO SA   OUR GRA   OUS U   N

Q62. The characters of the chess pieces

Her grandfather has been teaching Ermyntrude chess. She has firm ideas about the morality and character of the pieces. She thinks they are all rather nasty, always threatening and trying to push each other off the board. She also feels that the black and the white pieces ought to work together and be friends.

She dislikes some pieces more than others. She hates the subtle, deceiving knights with their sly, this-way that-way, jinking move. They do not make a straightforward threat, head on, like the honest rook, although she thinks *they* are rather aggressive.

Ermyntrude loves the King, who is quiet and dignified, moving sedately only one pace at a time and modestly keeps out of the way. She is fond of pawns, but questions their sly sideways attack. And she can't stand Queens. She thinks they are too powerful and bossy, threatening everyone in every direction and charging round the board upsetting things.

Bishops she really hates, ever since her grandfather took her Queen from the opposite corner with his Bishop. They are too devious for her, they attack unexpectedly from a flank, diagonally, and their threat reaches to the limit of the board. She says that they are also hypocrites – pretending to be religious, holy pieces, pieces of peace, while they strike aslant from afar.

Her grandfather took her up on the question of the Bishops. This was his question.

If there were any number of bishops, how many would be needed to threaten every square on the board? Spaces occupied by bishops must themselves be under threat. How should this number of bishops be placed?

Answer 72

Q63. Relationships

Visiting relations, of whom I have vast numbers, I often get confused.

'You *must* know whom I mean,' says Effie, who is a second cousin, I think. 'Her name was Gloria or Jane or something, and she is the daughter of the daily woman who used to be such a treasure to Poor Aunt Tabitha's eldest daughter. Or was it her cousin? You can't possibly have forgotten her! Or was it him? Anyway, it was her friend's sister's son I want to talk about. You know *him* of course.'

'Go on. Go on. I am dying to hear the details.'

You know the sort of thing. Relationships are complex, often hard to fathom. Try to fathom this one out. There is a relationship between the top two figures, and between the lower left hand figure and one of the other four. Which is it – A, B, C or D? Surely you *must* know.

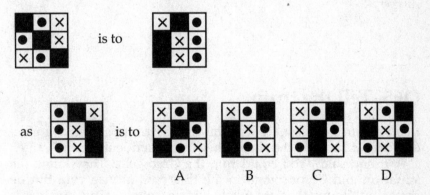

Answer 83

GO   SA   E OUR GRA   OUS   UEEN

93

Q64. How to put things right

My late beloved friend Marvin Grosswirth was far too witty. He, as Chairman of American Mensa, was on the platform with me as International Chairman at the time. We were in Vancouver, or Cleveland, or Tallahassee, or somewhere! It was a big meeting.

I tried to be amusing in my speech, but time and again he would cap every would-be funny story amid shouts of gleeful laughter. Finally, in utter frustration after a devastatingly witty sally from him, I shrugged helplessly and put my tongue out at him.

'Well put,' said Marvin.

Here is a question of putting. You have to put these words together to form just three words, using all eight segments.

MAN HE GET FIRE ANT SIT TO HER

Answer 94

Q65. Tell the truth

I had a sum to invest. I got a hint that a firm might have a take-over bid. If I bought the shares they might suddenly rise in value.

A friend said, 'You could ring the Gradwells. They know the situation and if you mention me they will advise you. But be careful. Although they are twins, John is a straight guy but Tom is a pathological liar.'

I had minutes to decide before my broker closed for the day. If Tom answered and I asked for John, he would say he *was* John, and give a wrong report. If I did get John, I would not know that I had. How did I safely get the right advice with only one call?

Answer 15

Q66. Symbolic magic

This is a symbol square and it is magic. The symbols in the top row are given. You have to complete the square, arranging the same five symbols in the remaining boxes so that every row, column and main diagonal has all five symbols.

Answer 26

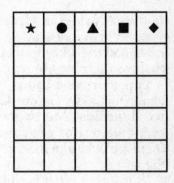

Q67. All the Ks

K	K	L	R	U	N	K	K
N	N	L	H	O	K	A	O
I	E	I	K	I	N	E	P
G	E	K	T	G	K	K	E
H	D	T	A	B	O	N	K
T	E	R	S	O	D	U	K
N	O	K	U	K	K	E	I
O	E	T	I	K	N	A	P

My friend, Ken Russell, set this for me. If you read anarch-ically, starting anywhere and going up or down, left or right, horizontally, vertically or dia-gonally, you might find many words in this square. But if I restrict you to words beginning with 'K', how many will you get?

Twenty points if you find them all.

Answer 37

GOD SAVE OUR GRACIOUS QUEEN

Q68. The majority below average?

In the early days of Mensa I had many calls from journalists who wanted to make a story, usually negative in those days. They often had the story in their mind already and asked me questions that would bring out remarks to support it.

One journalist called up and started talking enthusiastically about this new 'Genius Club'. I deprecated. 'You cannot use the word 'genius'. Mensa members have scored in the top two per cent on a test of general intelligence, so if we are geniuses then there are over a million geniuses in Britain, which rather devalues the term.'

'But surely, Sir, it is well known that the *vast* majority of people are *far* below average intelligence.'

'Well, statistically half of them would score *above* average, wouldn't they?'

The journalist rang off, his story ruined.

'What a fool,' I thought, and then changed my mind. There are, I began to see, ways of looking at humanity in which it is perfectly true to say that the vast majority are below average in some respect or again that the vast majority are above average in some respect.

Your problem is to find an example of each.

Answer 48

Q69. Classes in grammar

These six words fall into two classes – three in each – from the point of view of grammar. Can you sort them out and name the two classes to which they belong?

slowly, slightly, friendly, rapidly, spindly, carefully

Answer 59

Q70. Change letters, make a word

You have to change the first letter of each word in each column and you must leave six good English words in each column after the change. But, here is the problem. Your choice is restricted. You have to find a six-letter English word whose letters in sequence can be used to replace the first letters of the words in both columns going down the columns. In other words LGWCWL and KSBWSB must both be changed to the same word.

LICK	KIND
GRATE	STEM
WINE	BEAT
CHIN	WRAP
WAGER	SON
LIGHT	BOAR

Answer 7

Q71. Difficult definitions

This tale shows once again what a little horror I was at the age of ten.

There was a street orator talking to a Cockney audience on Beresford Square Market in Woolwich around 1922. A small lad in short trousers and a school cap, I was an avid listener as I chewed my apple.

'You blokes talk about socialism,' the speaker said to the work-men, ' but does any of you know what the word *means*? Do you? I ask you! Come on now, there's fifty of you here. I bet there is no one here who can *define* socialism. Come now. Anyone? You see. You don't know!'

At that point, in the piercing treble voice for which I was noted, I called out, 'Socialism, Sir, is defined as the nationalisation of the means of production, distribution and exchange.'

There was a laughing cheer from the crowd but the speaker, a professional, got the better of me with his witty repartee.

'Boy,' he shouted. 'Why don't you sling yer 'ook and get orf back to the Polytechnic?' I slung it, cheerfully chewing my apple, as the crowd laughed again.

It is one thing to know what a word means contextually, but it is another to be able to define it.

Here are some words and some definitions. There are more than enough definitions for your needs, and you have to select the correct definition for each word and write its number in the box provided.

☐ Neoplasm	1. Unprogressive	6. Angry
☐ Infatuated	2. Ruling	7. Madly in love
	3. Imperial	8. Bubbly
☐ Infinite	4. Unclear	9. Extremely large
☐ Retrogressive	5. Limitless	10. Redfaced
☐ Hegemony	11. Morbidly swollen	
☐ Inchoate	12. Reactive, retreating from advance	
	13. Leaden bluish coloured	
☐ Turbid	14. Leadership of a confederacy	
☐ Turgid	15. Unformed, just begun	
	16. Inspired with extravagant passion	
☐ Livid	17. Unexpected new tissue as in cancer	
☐ Genome	18. The entire set of chromosomes in a cell	

Answer 71

Q72. Connections

One of the feats of the human mind that is very difficult to simulate on computers is the solving of this kind of association problem. Philosophers have no idea how it is done.

You have to find a semantic connection between four phrases from utterly different contexts. The only connection is the linking word or idea. Here are four clues to four phrases linked by a single keyword. What is this keyword?

1. A stricken ball.
2. Hiding faults.
3. A cartoon beauty.
4. A large residence in the District of Columbia.

Answer 82

Q73. A well forgotten phrase

This scrambled quotation comes from a very famous politician. I heard it myself before World War II. I remember it because it was so striking, but I am sure that if he remembered it himself the speaker regretted it not many years later. Untangle it, please, and see if you can guess who said it.

> hatred philosophy bayonets night arctic Russia and proclaims starved lips mechanically through outcast sharpens death self her of self in her and her

Answer 93

P T TT   TA T   P T   TT   T

Q74. Names can be awkward

I claim to be 'nominally deprived'. My full name is Victor Vladimirovich Serebriakoff and when I was a small boy in an English poor district school in the thirties I would have given a lot to be Bill Jones. I was the butt of the class and the teachers too. Then I joined the army, and it was worse. A roll call went like this.

The corporal reading the list: 'Abrahams.'

'Sah!'

'Jenkins.'

'Sah!'

'Smith.'

'Sah!'

'Er . . . Ser – er –.'

'Sah!' I barked.

However, it sometimes worked to my advantage. When I was about twelve I was stopped on my bicycle by a policeman. 'Now then, young 'un. It's twenty minutes after lighting up time and you are *not* lit up. I'm afraid your name and address must be took.' He produced his pen and notebook and tapped the one on the other menacingly. 'Now then, your name, if you please.'

'Victor Vladimirovich Serebriakoff, Sir.'

He tapped his book again. There was a pause. 'Er – yes. Well, 'op it and watch it with the lights next time.'

Here are some famous names and a list of occupations. Can you fit the name with the occupation in each case?

1. T. S. Eliot	A. Mathematical Astronomer
2. Sir Karl Popper	B. Playwright
3. Dame Nellie Melba	C. Opera Singer
4. Pierre-Simon,	
Marquis de Laplace	D. Poet
5. Bonar Law	E. British politician
6. Sir Arthur Pinero	F. Cricketer
7. James Clerk Maxwell	G. Physicist
8. Jack Hobbs	H. Philosopher of science

Answer 14

Q75. It can be done

This is a kickself problem. It seems impossible but it is absurdly easy if you think straight and know your stuff.

The integers are the entire set of all the whole numbers. Write down, without calculation or hesitation, the product of all the integers up to 72. That is, just give the result of multiplying them all together.

Answer 25

Q76. A word ladder

Can you climb a seven-rung word ladder from SNAIL up to SHELL where every rung is a good English word. You may not change more than one letter at each rung.

| SHELL |
| |
| |
| |
| |
| |
| SNAIL |

Answer 36

P T	T TH	HT A	TH	P T	T TH	HT

Q77. A bright idea

This is true. As a skilled wood-machinist I was in a reserved occupation during World War II. I was popular with the men as the shop clown, but the foreman put me in the hated class of workers who were 'too clever' and insufficiently respectful.

I was given one of the hated boring jobs, cutting foundry wedges on a small bandsaw. They were three inches long, an inch thick, and tapered from half an inch to one eighth. You cross cut 1" x 6" board into 3" lengths and then, with a jig, cut the wedges, turning the stock piece over each time, as in the diagram.

The order was for forty sacks, enough desperately boring work for two months. It was a punishment job, reserved for those who displeased.

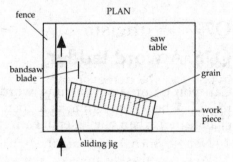

I worked out a way to do it much faster. Five days later I went back to the office asking for another job. The foreman sighed. 'Go back and finish them,' he instructed. 'I said forty sacks.'

'They are all finished.'

'Forty sacks?'

'Come and see!'

The foreman shrugged with weary scepticism and walked across to the machine. His eyes opened when he saw the rows of sacks and he was intensely suspicious. He spent some time checking the wedges and turning out a few sacks to see if they were full of sawdust underneath the top layer of wedges. Then he asked how I had managed it, and I showed him.

'Get the wedges to the foundry,' he said, 'and then get on the big moulder. Do the job the proper way next time.'

This may be an unfair question, but what was my bright idea?

Answer 47

Q78. A long word

What is the longest English word you can find which has in it these three letters, together or separated, in this order?

E   C   L

Answer 58

Q79. Scepticism

Religion involves faith, but science is based on scepticism, hypothesis and demonstration.

A Priest and a Scientist were walking in the country. It was a beautiful day. 'Ah!' said the Scientist. 'Just look at that flock of sheep on the hillside.'

'Newly shorn, I see,' said the Priest.

'Well, on this side anyway,' replied the Scientist.

Here are the names of some scientists who made very important contributions to human knowledge. One of them was also a priest. They include two chemists, a physiologist, a biochemist, a physicist, a mathematician and a biologist. Which is which, and what is the important contribution that each of them made?

John Dalton   Theodor Schwann
Gregor Mendel   Ernest Rutherford
Francis Crick   Claud Shannon
Dmitri Mendeleyev

Answer 69

P T   T TH   I HT AN   TH NP T   T TH   I HT

Q80. Daftypuz

This is a daft little puzzle. There are three pairs of short words to find from the clues, with the first and last letter supplied in each case. The answers have a feature in common. It is tricky stuff – are you up to it?

An eastern spiritual guide floors it?   G ? ? ?   ? ? G

A player's links record?   G ? ? ?   ? ? G

Southern bear is in order?   K ? ? ? ?   ? K

Answer 8

Q81. Another muddled aphorism

Your problem is a noble one. You have to distil great thoughts from jumbled nonsense.

Here are the words, debased and disordered, which put together properly by a skilled hand, are wise words for the wise. Put them straight, do!

> CORDIALLY   ROUGH   CLEVER   THE   BE   A   AS   AND
> FOR   THEMSELVES   RATHER   ORDINARY   DISLIKE
> MOST   PEOPLE   EACH   HATE   FOLK   PLACE   MUST
> THEM   FOR   THEY   OTHER   WORLD

Answer 81

Q82. More connections

What common swindle connects a high-up musician, 'nonsense!' and an urban conflagration pastime?

Answer 92

Q83. You are a contortionist – 1

During the London Blitz I was thirty, on skilled war work. I got tired of the close confinement, the smell and discomfort of our dugout in the garden with a large quarrelling family. I returned to my lovely bed on the top floor. OK, a bit of plaster fell once or twice and a window was blown in once. Nevertheless, I learned to sleep through the AA barrage, which made much more noise than the occasional high flying sneak raider.

But one night I was filled with joy which suddenly turned to fear. It was about two o'clock. I heard a raider with a slightly different sound, just audible through the barrage. Then the noise of the raider's engine stopped. 'Got 'im!' I shouted joyfully, assuming the AA or a fighter had hit the raider. Then came a shaking explosion nearby as the plane hit the town and its bombs went off. The same thing happened again. And again. And again.

'They are knocking them down like a pigeon shoot,' I joyfully cried. But when the fifth went down my heart suddenly misgave. This was too good to be true. These were something new – pilotless planes as I later discovered. It was the first night of the buzzbombs that chugged impassively across from France, then suddenly stopped their engines and dived to destroy you.

It went on all night. I went down to the shelter again. I was

P TO TTH L HT AN TH NP TO TTH L HT

105

irreligious, but that night I prayed.

Which brings me circuitously to my puzzle – a Kickself problem.

Put your hands before you in a normal praying attitude, finger tips together. Now if you are normally fit you will find that, holding your palms together and lifting your elbows, you can rotate your hands – keeping them palm to palm – a full 360 degree turn until you have the finger tips together again. You finish with your right hand to the left and your left hand to the right, still palm to palm.

You have made one complete revolution with your palms in full contact all the time. Could you turn any more? Could you complete two continuous revolutions? Yes, you can!

I am an old man with rheumy joints but, without distortion or hurting myself – starting palm to palm and without parting my hands – I can make two complete revolutions, bringing finger tips to finger tips twice more after the start. There is no trick. How do I do it?

I shall make you a contortionist because you can do it, when you know how. But can you work out how to do it for yourself?

Answer 13

Q84. You are a contortionist – 2

You will kick yourself if you fail!

Take a piece of cord about two feet long and hold both ends firmly. Now without letting go of either end, tie a knot in the cord.

It can be done. It is so simple! But can you work out how?

Answer 24

Q85. Make do and mend

The main problem of any army in training is to occupy the day. Young male recruits have to be kept busy all the time or there will be troubles of many kinds. That is the job of the NCO.

One time-filler we quite enjoyed after the exercises and drilling was called 'Make Do and Mend' – a session of stitching, darning and patching your personal effects. But while we were at it we were amusing one another with catches and puzzles.

Corporal Stein gave the squad this. 'A good soldier must make do. In the field you will be short of everything and you will have to use what is around whether it is intended for the purpose or not.

'This sentence has shell holes in it. You have to fill the gaps with the same seven letters, which is all you've got. Letters will be used in the same order each time, according to King's Regs. Your completed sentence has to make sense.'

'This is the sentence:

THE (gap) DOCTOR WAS (gap) TO OPERATE BECAUSE THERE WAS (gap).

'Right! On the command 'Start', start. Squad, Start!'

I solved it quickly enough but you've got to give the sergeant and the lance-jack a chance, so I kept quiet. I was in enough trouble for winning all the squad's pay at brag the previous night.

The sergeant, with the help of Private Scott and half the squad, finally got it, which put him in a good mood. Good for us all.

But can you get it?

Answer 35

PUT OUT TH L   HT AND TH N PUT OUT TH L   HT

Q86. Use all you've got

Tommy Butterworth and Teddy Johnson, the clever ones who had been sent out of their mixed ability class to study on their own, were fiddling with calculators instead of reading for their GCSE mocks the next week.

'I've got a fab puzzle for you,' said Tommy. 'Betcha can't do it in an hour. My dad says that in this life you've got to use all you've got. My calculator has ten number keys, and I want you to use each of them once only in conjunction with any of the other keys so that you come to a result of 12 on the display.'

Teddy said 'Easy peasy', and worked away for a time. 'Hard pard,' he eventually said, 'it can't be done.'

'Can too, dim wit!'

They fell to enjoyable scuffling.

Can it be done, and if so, how?

Answer 46

Q87. Multiply to reverse

There is a five-digit integer which when multiplied by four is simply reversed (vwxyz becomes zyxwv, so to speak). There is but one answer. Can you find it?

Answer 57

Q88. Misunderstanding foreigners

In the sixties, deep in the Cold War, the British and Russian delegations at the International Standards Organisation were at the same table at the Ukraina, that dreadful wedding-cake hotel in Moscow.

Nitchkov, the leader of the Russian delegation, asked my name. On hearing the answer he roared and said 'Migod! The Chief by the British delegation is only a Russian!' He translated to the others, who roared excessively. But they shyly liked me.

The Chairman and the Secretariat were Russian and the meeting was chaos because they had no idea of the usual rules of order at meetings. When amendments and points of order were raised there was Russian puzzlement and shrugs with indignant confusion among all the other delegations. It went on hopelessly for hours. I leaned across to Nitchkov and said, 'How do you Russians like presiding over this Noah's Ark of incomprehension?'

'Belgian Airlines,' he said.

I said that he must have misheard or misunderstood my question, and repeated it slowly.

'I understood you, Victor Vladimirovich,' he grinned. 'I still say Belgian Airlines – Sabena.'

'But I don't follow.'

Nitchkov laughed, said 'Sabena' again and counting out the letters of the word on his fingers said 'Such A Bloody Experience! Never Again!'

This set me thinking about other 'phrase-words' based on airline names. TWA could be 'Try Walking Across'. Here is a clue to a phrase based on LUFTHANSA: 'Try not to remember that dislike and ill nature are everywhere'.

Can you find the phrase?

Answer 68

PUT OUT THE LIGHT AND THEN PUT OUT THE LIGHT

Q89. More connections

Here is another of those wretched 'if this is to that what are those to the other' questions.

Some clever people cannot do them at all. Are you one of them, or can your solve it?

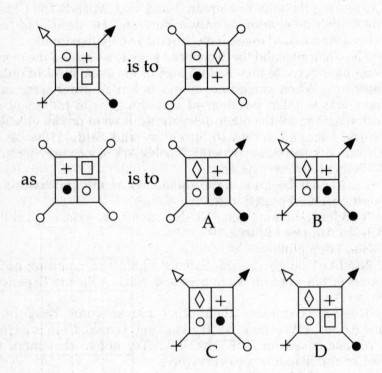

Answer 79

Q90. Robust politeness

I listen with delight to the British parliamentary debates on radio and TV. No one ever says anything is 'untrue' – it is 'not the case'. MPs who are also Privy Councillors are addressed as 'Right Honourable' even when, in indirect language, they are being blackguarded unmercifully.

'The Right Honourable Gentleman will of course remember . . .', when the speaker is certain that he does not remember.

But Margaret Thatcher was often more robustly polite. My joy was to hear her shout in tones that rang from the vault, 'The Right Honourable Gentleman, with all due respect, is a blundering amateur.'

A blundering amateur would have little chance with this tricky puzzle. Even a competent professional might have a problem.

There are many fifth order magic squares, yet composing one of them is a tall order. Below you will find a square with some of the boxes filled in. You have to fill in the rest. Remember, all the columns, the rows, and the main diagonals must add up to the same constant.

You need fast figuring and clear logic. It is trial and error. The best of luck!

15		23		11
9		22		5
3		16		24

Answer 9

N   N   A P OP   A , A   A   O

Q91. The duel

Kurt Kwizzer and James Riddell were deadly rivals at the puzzle game. They were puzzle setters who were constantly stealing and adapting each other's puzzles and desperately competing for publication.

Friends brough them together to effect a reconciliation, but they refused to shake hands and stared at each other furiously. Despite friendly cajoling neither would speak to the other. Kurt said to one of their mutual friends, 'I shall not be the first to speak.'

'I am quite ready to accept Kwizzer's apologies,' said Riddell to another friend, 'otherwise I have nothing to say to the unpleasant man.' There was a long pause. Neither was willing to be the first to leave or the first to speak. Their friends were embarrassed, and wished they had never thought of such an idea.

Finally, Riddell seized a note pad, scribbled this upon it, and thrust it at Kwizzer.

<u>STAND</u>   <u>TAKE</u>   <u>TO</u>   <u>TAKINGS</u>
  I   YOU   THROW ALL MY

Kurt Kwizzer went white with rage and wrote this below.

<u>FIE! TENDITO</u>   EVERYOUYTHING
    TAKE

And so it went on until several sheets of paper were full.

James: SULTYOU AREING

Kurt: $\dfrac{\text{STAND ME?}}{\text{TENDIIT}}$

James: MYTRUWHYDEAFFAIRS?

Kurt: $\dfrac{\text{TENDITO}}{\text{AWE YOU BECAUSE I AABOMTE YOU}}$

James: $\dfrac{\text{SIIST}}{\text{SATISFACTION}}$

Kurt: $\dfrac{\text{THE BLASTED OAK}}{\text{THE}\quad\text{TOMORROW}\quad\text{FIELD THE CHURCH DAWN}}$

What I ask you, in blazes, were they on about? Can you translate their childish code?

Answer 91

Q92. Obstacle cricket

It was Lady Pamela's idea. She knew the professor played cricket well. She prepared a new, daft idea – 'obstacle cricket', a very impractical joke.

The steel wickets were fixed so that they could not fall and the bails were welded on. The oversize oval ball was full of lead and the curved bat was made of reinforced concrete. There was a tangled mass of rope-work behind both wickets.

Lady Pamela bet the professor a Rolls that he could neither score 20 nor bowl her out at 'obstacle cricket'.

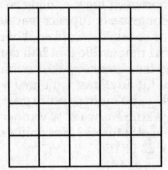

Here is a 5 x 5 word square, into which the same five words will fit reading both across and down. In the following paragraph are hidden synonyms, in order, of the five words. Can you find them and fit them in?

'Corny' tried to bowl, then to hurl, but finally had to heft the heavy ball like a shot-put. He got into a tangle as he ran up to bowl, and only managed to keep bowling for four changes of end. He won, but Lady Pamela had to default on her absurd bet. 'I was only joking,' she claimed. Such jokes!

Answer 20

N V   N W A P OP   A ,WA   W A   O

Q93. Winning when you can't play

At a slum school in the twenties I was unskilled at marbles, but still came out the winner. I have already admitted my covetous crimes as a ruthless marbles tycoon at a 'council school' in the thirties. There was more to my unsporting, grasping ways. Always inventive, I made up my own game – artful little beast that I was.

My game was this. Two boys contributed three marbles each. The two contestants were placed about ten feet apart behind chalk lines on the playground. The six stake marbles were placed in a line in the centre, between the two players.

Taking turns, the contestants flipped marbles from their own end trying to hit any of the stake marbles. What they hit they kept and they also recovered the marble that had connected. If they hit more than one marble they claimed all those that had been hit. A marble which did not hit anything remained where it ended up, and was then available to be hit in a future go.

How did I manage to be always a winner when I was less skilful than most of the other boys? How did I use common sense to overcome lack of skill?

Answer 30

Q94. Another phrase-word

I give you a clue to a phrase which is formed from the letters of the phrase-word, which is the name of an airline, in this case 'OLYMPIC'.

Clue: 'Olive was a pretty and rather kindly waitress in a depressed area. She used to let some of the unemployed young men have a meal 'on tick'. When the manageress found out she told her to stop allowing credit. What did she say?

Answer 40

Q95. Making your points

By putting a dot at each angle of this triangle, you have three lines of two dots. You have made each dot serve more than once.

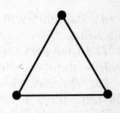

Now take ten dots, and arrange them so that they make four straight lines, each of four dots.

Answer 50

Q96. A frequent business lie

Starting at the correct square and reading any which way, moving from square to touching square, you should be able to find the most frequent business lie in writing.

I	N	H	E	C
T	S	T	E	H
H	I	E	U	Q
E	P	O	S	T

Answer 60

N V R N W ATP OP SA ,WAT W ATT O

Q97. Square the difference

Lady Pamela Swot was having breakfast in bed with Professor Kalkalus.

The man-servant had cleared away, and they were quarrelling mildly about the theory of surds.

Pamela said, 'Be a dear and get me my cigars and lighter from the table there. I crave a drag.'

'You know I hate tobacco and loathe cigar smoke.'

'Ah, men! You have your evil way with us and then deny us the slightest indulgence. Truly, after such sweet pleasure I need the weed. Do indulge me.'

'I'll not stir to bring you a drug which hurts your health.'

'Bet you will, Corny!'

'I simply and permanently refuse!'

'Well, solve this puzzle. If you fail, you indulge me.'

'You know I can easily solve all your simple-minded puzzles.'

'Select two different integers such that the difference between the integer and its square shall be the same with both integers. Wait! That is not all. Show me a principle by which one can select any number of such pairs.'

The professor thought for a bit. 'It cannot be done in bed,' he said, 'nor anywhere else I suspect.'

'You are usually so good in bed. It is a simple hard-think puzzle. You can do it in bed or not at all.'

'Prove that!'

'If I do, a nice Corona Corona to put me in a sweet mood?'

'You'll never prove it.'

Did she do it? Can it be done? Did she subject the professor to passive smoking again?

Answer 70

Q98. Another scrambled quotation

Here is a distorted, epigrammatic, poetic tombstone inscription for the architect Sir John Vanbrugh. Kindly decipher.

SIR JOHN VANBRUGH'S READER HOUSE UNDER SURVEY
HEAVY HE EARTH MANY A LIE LAID THEE FOR LOAD
CLAY THIS OF ON ON STONE DEAD HEAVY HIM

Answer 80

Q99. Same across, same down

Take a triplet of As, two pairs of Es, a couple of Ls, a pair of Ps, a brace of Ns, plus an R, an S and a T. With them make a crossword where the four downs and the four acrosses are the same four words.
   If you can!

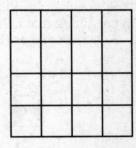

Answer 90

NEVER   ND W AT PEOP E SA ,WAT   W AT T E DO

Q100. Spotting faulty boxes

Caroline had drawn up the plans for a decorative box. This is how the unfolded boxes would look.

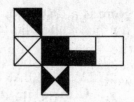

The foreman, however, was a bit of an artist and chafed about making things exactly to someone else's design all the time. He saw a chance to be creative, and introduced some similar but different designs for the boxes. Who would notice? The answer is Caroline. She would.

When she saw them in use at the annual display she spoke to the foreman. 'Your chaps have got it wrong on some of those boxes, haven't they?'

'They are all exactly to specification.' He spoke with great certitude, which often works well for foremen.

Caroline laughed. 'Come off it, Mr Boston. It doesn't matter, but some of them are not to drawing.'

'Are you going to make a fuss about it?'

'No. I just wanted you to know I knew.'

He half smiled with stern affection and touched her hand. 'You're a sharp-eyed one. But you'll make a designer yet. See you in the dining room. I'll stand you lunch.'

So, which of these boxes are not to plan?

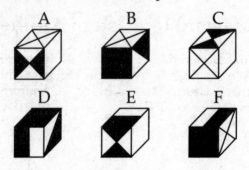

Answer 100

118

Q101. Square up to this

My first is this, my second is that and my third is the other. That was the form of some nineteenth century riddles. I use it about a word square to go in this frame.

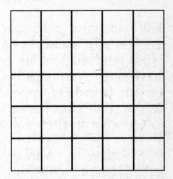

Five words, the same down as across, make up the word square.

Here is your cryptic clue. I hope you cannot solve it!

The ultimate military rank has 'my first'. A tasty meal has 'my second'. The leader of a band of noisy people may use 'my first' to get 'my third' from his followers. 'My fourth' is a certain character, an Ionic type, always last. 'My fifth' describes an organ; if you blow it you will make 'my third' or you can use it to check whether your tasty meal has 'my second'.

Answer 111

Q102. Phraseword for Eastern Airlines

I have already mentioned the well-known phraseword for TWA – 'Try Walking Across'. This time you must find a phrase for the American airline 'Eastern'. Your clue is: 'A limited number of eastern flights is now permitted'.

Answer 122

NEVER MIND WHAT PEOPLE SAY, WATCH WHAT THEY DO

Q103. Altered synonyms and antonyms

Here are four groups of six words. Each group has little connection as it stands but a slight alteration, a single letter in each word, and matters are very different. If you can do it you will have three synonyms (words of similar meaning) and three antonyms (words of opposite meaning) in each group (e.g. Jump, leap, vault – stop, freeze, stand).

See what an alteration one letter can make!

1.	Mate	Adobe	Score	Warship	Retest	Lose
2.	Grant	Vase	Greet	Punt	Shanty	Stall
3.	Full	Might	Glazing	Dumb	Grab	Fright
4.	Mood	Door	Brave	Mind	Must	Lad

Answer 133

Q104. Throw the odd ones out!

Here are three rows of figures. Each row would form a logical series if it were not for my mischievous tampering. One number from each row has been slipped into another row.

It is your job to detect the impostor in each row, and to work out into which row it should be moved in order to complete a series.

A. 0, 6, 110, 143, 323, 667

B. 24, 35, 72, 210, 288, 420

C. 0, 6, 20, 42, 72, 120, 156

Answer 144

Q105. What? More connections?

What connects a nominal oversize Yankee pippin, a cathedral in the North of England, a Royal air fighter, a difficult ball for a batsman to cope with, and an unboiled pudding eaten with beef?

There is a short word which connects all these things. What is it and what are the connections?

Answer 155

Q106. Department of trivial knowledge

How many of these questions can you get right without the use of any reference books?

Answers

1. What nut gives its flavour to marzipan?
2. Which mythical character flew too close to the sun?
3. What do the Greeks mean by 'pita'?
4. What is the capital of Outer Mongolia?
5. What were the two previous names of Istanbul?
6. Eva Braun had the briefest marriage. To whom?
7. What is measured by a barometer?
8. Where did Lady Godiva ride, covered only by her hair?
9. What is the 'pons asinorum'?
10. El-Alamein was a tiny empty settlement. Where is it and why is it famous?

Answer 166

C   DE   E   D CE,   E C   E   D E E

Q107. Finding an old friend unexpectedly

3	3	1	3	1	4
3	1	4	1	3	1
4	1	5	3	1	4
1	5	9	3	1	4
1	5	9	2	3	?

What digit, may I ask, should replace the question mark at the bottom right-hand corner of this rectangle?

Answer 177

Q108. Black and white

This puzzle poses lots of questions for you.

Can the big cube be assembled from a number of the smaller double cubes, or will an extra single cube be needed? If it is, what colour would it have to be?

And how many of the double cubes do you require?

Answer 124

Q109. Continued sustainable growth

Polly Titian, the Shadow Minister for Affairs, was once again in full flood.

'We hear nothing from all sides but demands for more 'growth'. Without much more 'growth' – by which we mean even more productivity, more production, more sales, more business, more activity, more consumption, more raids on the environment, more wealth for everyone (in rich countries) and therefore more tax revenue – the industrial nations will fall apart.

'I beg leave to doubt that perpetual growth, in the rich world, is either obtainable or desirable. We are on a treadmill: to get more productivity without unemployment we must all produce and *consume* more. *Can* people in the rich world continue to demand more and more and more goods and services? Is there not a law of diminishing returns? Will they have enough time to negotiate for, to buy, and to enjoy the ever increasing flood of goods and services?'

The Minister's reply was brief. 'I am sure my Honourable Friend is aware that 'Continued Sustainable Growth' is not only possible but essential and in the interests of all concerned.'

Can you achieve 'Continued Sustainable Growth'? You have to start with a single letter, and sustain growth by adding one letter at a time until you have reached an eight-letter word. This word signifies what sharp weapons should be. Each time you add a letter you must create a new word, and the letters must remain in the same order throughout the exercise.

You start with the letter 'A'. But can you sustain growth until eight letters are reached?

Answer 140

C DE   E UD CE, E C   E UD E E T

Q110. Head transplants

Modern surgery is advancing so fast that we shall soon be seeing head transplants. A person with a terminal brain disease will donate a useless but healthy body to another who is sound above the neck but about to die of a bodily illness. The social, religious, moral and personal implications are bizarre, to say the least.

In anticipation of this feat we can practice with words. Behead all fourteen words in the two lists below and replace the severed letter with another letter which will create a new word. But hold on a second. That is not all. You must use the same letter for each pair of words, and the seven letters which you use in total for the seven pairs must form a word, reading downwards.

What is this word?

SAND	BANG
BATH	CAST
BAKE	PACE
STEM	TON
CAMP	MALE
BIDE	SKIN
SANK	DAWN

Answer 110

Q111. Another airline phraseword

Here is the clue to a sentence where the words begin with the successive letters of 'AIR FRANCE'.

Clue: 'Everyone consumes wonderful meals in France and its neighbouring countries.'

What is the phrase?

Answer 101

124

Q112. Connections

Imaginary small workers, marvellous ancient structures, mortal crimes and what a 'heavy roller' likes to throw: they are all connected by an odd prime.

What is the connecting word and what are the references?

Answer 112

Q113. So square this one away, then

Clues to the five words, the same across as down, can be found (by the astute) in the following passage. So fill in five words across and five words down – five gets you ten!

It was 1750 and Sir James was in a hurry to get to 'first word'. He took his 'fifth word', which was faster than the stage. His groom fitted a special box to his saddle because Sir James would never be parted from his beloved Japanese pet 'third word'. Aboard the cross-channel packet he was deafened by the first mate's roar at two seamen as the vessel was about to 'fourth word' from the harbour. ' 'Second word'! yer lousy lubbers! Leave the tops'l be.'

Answer 123

C NDE N P E UD CE,   E C   E UD E ENT

Q114. Shattered crossword

The second law of thermodynamics says that all order dissipates, every complex ordered arrangement tends to get more mixed up with time. All ordered systems such as living things have to be repaired and renewed while they live, although they all decay and die in the end. And what repairs and renews is life itself. Living systems are in a constant war with the Second Law that randomises everything in time.

The Second Law seems to have been at work on this perfectly orderly crossword puzzle. It is now shattered and dispersed. Can you act for the Life Force by restoring and repairing it?

You can photocopy the poor broken thing, cut it up, and solve it like a jigsaw puzzle, or you can fill in the letters and blank squares in the grid provided.

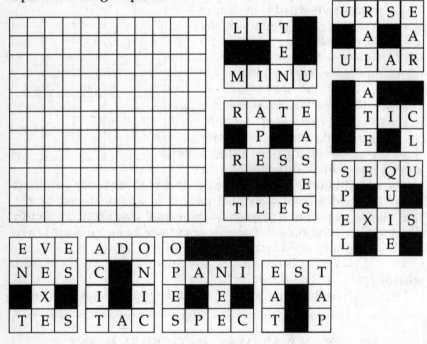

Answer 134

126

Q115. You have no imagination

Lady Pamela Swot and Professor Cornelius Kalkalus were riding. It was a sunny day but the turf on the Kentish downs after recent rains was good. Lady Pam said as they cantered along, 'This is the style of life mankind was bred for.'

'Nonsense,' said the Professor. 'Breeding implies purpose; but evolution knows nothing of purpose, it only knows what survives. The stockbreeder that bred these nags knew what he was looking for. We were bred for any lifestyle which is sustainable.'

'Poor old Corny,' retorted Lady Pam. 'You are a wonderful mathematician but you have no imagination.'

'There you go again! Down we come from the general to personalities. What a bore! Mathematics, more than any other form of thought, calls for imagination. The whole of the realm of mathematics is imaginary.'

'I still say, my dearest man, that you have no imagination.'

They had relaxed to a trot after a long canter, and the horses were blowing a bit. Pamela reigned in under a beautiful may tree which was in full blossom in a small valley by a tiny stream.

'I can prove to you that you have no imagination,' she claimed.

'Mathematicians demand proof.'

'Imagine a square of paper, about six inches square.'

'About 150mm, yes.'

'Imagine folding it in two at right angles.'

'What a strain! My imagination is working overtime.'

'Now fold it once more, the other way. What have you?'

'A square, Miss Simplicity.'

'Now take a pair of imaginary scissors and cut through diagonally, from the solid corner to the loose corner.'

'The imaginary deed is done.'

'Unfold and what is the result? How many pieces are there, and what shapes?'

The Professor thought for a while and then said, 'Look, I thought

CONDE N P EJUD CE,   E CO E JUD E ENT

we were supposed to be riding. Bet I beat you to that copse along the stream.' And he was away at a gallop. Despite his unfair start, Lady Pamela almost caught him up.

The Professor had avoided answering the questions. Now it is your turn. As an unfair advantage the illustration below shows the folding and cutting. Can you answer Lady Pamela's questions from your imagination alone? How many pieces will there be and of what shape?

Draw your answer in the space provided.

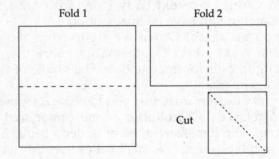

Your answer:

Answer 145

Q116. The riddle of the Sphinx

Riddles, puzzles and enigmas go back to Babylon and beyond. Every reader will remember how Oedipus saved Thebes by solving the riddle of the Sphinx. But on the chance that you don't remember the riddle, or if you do you don't remember the answer, I am giving this vintage puzzle again.

Can you equal the mighty Oedipus? What creature, he was asked, goes on four legs at dawn, on two feet at bright midday and on three feet when the sun goes down?

Think carefully before you solve this. Oedipus saved Thebes and broke the power of the Sphinx by his solution, but it did him nothing but harm. The seeming 'reward' was the hand in marriage of the royal widow, Jocasta. But she turned out to be his own mother and the outcome of the incestuous match was total tragedy, Greek tragedy.

Answer 156

Q117. Rank these prefixes

Below is a list of prefixes to units of measurement in the SI system. For instance, we have kilometres and millimetres. The list is arranged in order, but the wrong order – alphabetical. Can you rearrange them in order of magnitude, rising from the minute to the enormous?

> atto, centi, deca, deci, femto, giga, hecto,
> kilo, mega, micro, milli, nano, pico, tera

Answer 167

Q118. Keep that pencil on the paper

At the Puzzle Masters' Convention it was inevitable that Kurt Kwizzer and James Riddell should be brought together. They circulated talking to friends, each with a wary hating eye upon the other, trying to avoid a confrontation.

But the press were there, and a confrontation was just what they wanted. Fred Flare of *The Morning Smirch* went to Kwizzer while Susy Sobber of *The Weekly Slander* went to Riddell, both with the same tale. There was this new puzzler who was very quick. Would they like to see him?

They were brought together on the platform and publicly challenged to be the first to solve this puzzle. Neither would shake hands, neither would back down. They were forced to compete, much against their will. They were each given a red pencil and a white board, with this design of dots on it.

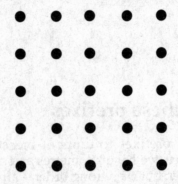

The challenge was, and is for you, to draw as few straight lines as possible to pass through all the dots, without taking the pencil off the board.

Answer 178

Q119. An addled quotation

Here is a quotation, a variant on a more usual one. You have all the letters and they are in the right order but muddled in the rows. Award yourself an extra point if you can remember the popular pianist who said it.

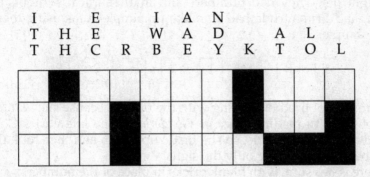

```
I     E       I   A   N
T   H E       W   A D     A L
T   H C   R   B   E Y   K T O L
```

Answer 160

Q120. More connections

What is the link between filthy lucre, what Aaron made behind Moses' back, the way into a Greek-Turkish Sea, and what Jason stole and the Argonauts recovered?

Answer 102

H   II   I   HI G   F

131

Q121. Placing digits

You will remember Ermyntrude Eunous, the absurdly clever small girl who was introduced in my poem in a previous puzzle (Q31).

One day Ermyntrude was playing with a set of mathematical bricks which Mrs Teresa Char, her 'special needs' teacher, had brought her. They had numbers and mathematical symbols on them, and Ermyntrude had to make up simple sums using them. For example:

But she got tired of playing with the bricks because she wanted to get on with reading *Alice in Wonderland*. She knew Mrs Char could not resist a puzzle, so she made up a sum and then took the numbers away leaving only the signs.

Here is her sum, with blank bricks in place of the numbers:

☐ ☐ ☐ x ☐ + ☐ ☐ ☐ = ☐ ☐ ☐

'Mrs Char,' she said, 'I have taken the numbers away from this sum and I can't remember where they go. Please can you put them back in their proper place?'

She pointed to the group of bricks which she had removed. The group was made up of the numbers 1, 2, 3, 4, 5, 6, 8 and two 0s.

'Would you put them back in place, Mrs Char,' she begged. 'I know you can, you know such a lot.'

It worked like a charm. Mrs Char was busy for an hour and a half while the little girl eagerly read her book.

Can you fill in the blanks, and can you do it in less than an hour and a half?

Answer 121

Q122. Snap chances

Harold Farquarson and Cecil Beaufort were at a weekend party at Beaufort Towers during the holidays. The weather was awful and the younger children, Zoe and Ned, were persistently playing snap with two decks of cards, while Lord Beaufort was half asleep in an armchair.

Harold said, 'I think snap is the most boring game in the world.'

'Do you think so?' replied Cecil. 'They seem to enjoy it.'

'That is their limited intelligence. What is the sense of a game where almost every play is a nullity?'

Lord Beaufort looked at them over his glasses. 'You dismal young swots have no idea,' he said. 'You should not insult the young ones, they are bright enough. Snap is a good old game.'

Cecil said, 'They play hundreds of pairs of cards before they get the thrill of a pair.'

'Nothing of the kind,' retorted Lord Beaufort. 'I have been watching, and they get a snap chance about once in a hundred plays.'

'Not so! It's hundreds and hundreds,' cried his son.

Harold intervened. 'No, sir, you're both wrong. I'll bet a pound they get a snap before they finish going through the pack once, i.e. fifty two plays.'

'Take him up, Father,' cried Cecil. 'He hasn't a chance! It will teach him not to be so cock-sure.'

The children were excited by the bet, which Harold won. They played another round at Lord Beaufort's insistence, and Harold was proved right again. Indeed, although he lost some and won some, by the end of the afternoon and several dozen games Harold was £27 ahead.

What are the chances of a 'snap' in a run of 52 plays?

Answer 132

H MI I   I NO HING O   O   OF

Q123. Spot spotting

Kurt Kwizzer had thought of a new kind of puzzle. He knew that his arch rival, James Riddell, was very good at normal forms of puzzle but a bit flummoxed by anything novel. Hoping to publicly humiliate his rival he called Fred Flare of *The Morning Smirch*. He immediately rang his girlfriend, Susy Sobber, of *The Weekly Slander*. They got James to an office party on the pretext of an introduction to the features editor to arrange a commission for a series of puzzles.

By arrangement, when Riddell arrived there was a crowd around Kwizzer. He was demonstrating his new puzzle which was displayed on the wall on a large chart, thus:

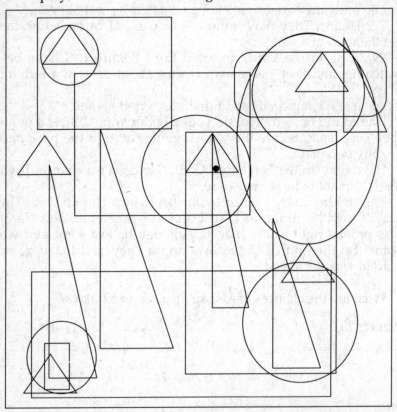

'Here you have,' he was saying, in his faint Viennese accent, 'a complex layout which can be thought of as a Venn diagram, where the various overlapping shapes indicate class membership.

'What matters is where a spot may be in relation to the figures that surround it or do not surround it. One spot is shown. There are just two other locations with similar contexts where a spot could logically be placed. The task is to identify and mark the exact point at which the two other spots should be placed.'

Riddell was fascinated in spite of himself but feigned lack of interest as he chatted with Susy about the supposed commission.

The newsroom staff were making wild wrong guesses, grabbing Kurt's pointer to show where the spots could be. James could hear the monotonous 'No, not there!' again and again from Kwizzer.

He had been studying the chart surreptitiously and suddenly left Susy, walked across the room and said confidently, 'May I have the baton, please, Mr Kwizzer.' He was almost polite.

Kwizzer went pale. He was nervous. 'If it will be of use to you, Mr Riddell,' he said.

'Obviously, there,' said Riddell as he stabbed, 'and there,' as he stabbed again. He knew he was right when Kwizzer snapped 'A silly journalistic plot,' and walked from the room, taking a glass of wine and a *vol-au-vent* as he went.

Considering *he* had approached the press, his complaint was implausible.

Where did Riddell point? Mark your own two dots in the appropriate locations on the drawing opposite.

Answer 143

H MI IT I NOTHING TO   O D OF

Q124. Crossword jigsaw

As in Q114, here is a complete crossword which has been cut up like a jigsaw puzzle into sixteen pieces. Can you use them to complete the grid provided? Or you could photocopy them, and piece them together like a jigsaw.

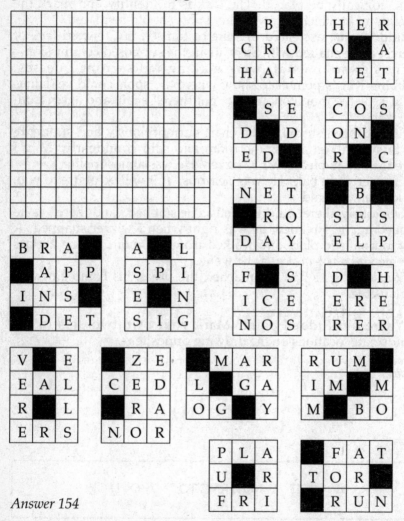

Answer 154

136

Q125. Shrimpoas 2

'Shrimpoas', you will remember, is an anagram or mix-up of 'aphorisms'. Here are the great thoughts of great men, with the words and the author's name deliberately muddled.

Disentangle them if you can, and write your answer below each line.

1. ARE AVOIDED TO VULGAR BE WILDE THEY CONVINCING ARE ARGUMENTS ALWAYS AND OFTEN

2. MORE SHAKESPEARE APPAREL FASHION WEARS THE MAN OUT THAN

3. THERE ARE JOHNSON RUDENESS UPON WHICH ALL APOLOGY IS OCCASIONS

Answer 165

Q126. I, thief, confess

What I stole from her she still had, hating it. But when I asked her to return what she detested, she refused – amazed at my effrontery. I even offered to give her back what I had stolen and more besides for compensation, but she refused with passionate indignation. What was the stolen property?

Answer 176

H MILIT I NOTHING TO B P O D OF

Q127. Get this square

The word square comprises five words, the same down as across. The paragraph below provides the clues to solve it. The missing words, referred to as 'first word', 'second word', etc, fit into the square reading from top to bottom, and from left to right.

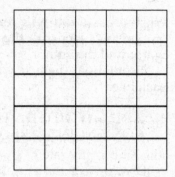

Clue: 'Aphrodite alighted in a beautiful Greek grove. It was so entrancing that she lingered for the fruit. But she got 'first word' waiting for the 'second word's to 'third word'. The odds are 'fourth word' that the fruit will be too 'fifth word' to eat for a month.'

Answer 179

Q128. Another resuscitated riddle

Here is another example of a very old riddle.
   'What is the difference between a cat and a comma?'
   Answer: one has claws at the end of its paws, and the other has a pause at the end of its clause.

   So now tackle this one: 'What is the difference between a speared lion and a very wet day?'

Answer 170

Q129. The statistical approach

The Professor and Lady Pamela were riding with another friend, Dr Gauss, and again they spotted a flock of sheep on the downland hillside.

Dr Gauss remarked on the sheep. 'Fine Wiltshire Whites, I think.'

Lady Pam, hoping to create an argument, mischievously said again 'And shorn I see.'

The Professor, recognising his cue, grinned and said, 'Well, on this side at any rate.'

Dr Gauss, a statistician, said, 'I think we can go further than that.' He counted. 'There are 20 sheep and ten of them are facing one way and ten the other. We can estimate the probability of the hypothesis that they are all unshorn on the side we cannot see, or the probability of the other hypothesis that any individual sheep is unshorn on the invisible side.'

Can we? If we can, what are these probabilities?

Answer 119

Q130. Coping with the unknown again

Harold Farquarson and Cecil Beaufort, the clever public school-boys, were skulking at the Farquarson home. Sir Quentin and Lady Ellen, Harold's parents, were golfing and the boys had been commanded to go for a bracing walk round to see how the hares and pheasants were fattening against a shoot.

But the idle lads were in Sir Quentin's study. Cecil was absorbed

HUMILITY IS NOTHING TO BE PROUD OF

in Sir Quentin's library, while Harold was plotting a puzzle that he hoped Cecil would not be able to solve.

Eventually he said, 'Sissy! I have a problem you will never do!'

'Don't call me that, Hal, or I shall transcombabulate you.'

'Define that verb!'

'Call me that again, and you will learn its meaning empirically.'

'Define that absurd adverb.'

'By bitter experience.'

'You've just read it in a dictionary. Now then, Cecil, I bet you a quid you can't do my puzzle.'

'Let's see it.'

Harold produced the following, and said in an imitation of their maths teacher's voice, 'Fill in the missing totals and find the values of W, X, Y and Z.'

W	Y	X	Y	?
X	X	Z	W	24
Z	Y	W	X	29
W	Z	Z	Y	33
27	31	28	?	

Cecil said, 'Oh, that sort of puzzle. Make it two quid and I'll bother.'

'Done!'

But Cecil spent a long time on it, and moaned and groaned when he finally cracked it.

'You cheated,' he claimed. 'I thought they were integers.'

'No,' said Harold, 'you made an unwarranted assumption. But you did solve it eventually. So here is my I.O.U.'

'Another? I have a pocketful already.'

What was the answer?

Answer 103

Q131. Fit integers into Venn diagram

The primary and most important task for the newborn child, as for the adult, is classification. Everything, looked at closely enough, is unique. For the human mind to deal with the vast variety of things, we have to put them into sets or classes, where the members are sufficiently alike for some purpose.

But Nature is messy. Lots of things belong to several classes and that creates muddle. The Venn diagram helps us to understand messy sets or classes where they overlap. For instance, a dog is an animal, a mammal, a carnivore, a canine, a domestic animal, and so on. It belongs to all these classes at once.

This puzzle deals with numbers. For instance, 7 is an integer, it is also a prime number, and it belongs to the set of odd numbers. The set of integers, the whole numbers, is large – but it is small in comparison with the enormous set of 'real' numbers (the fractional ones).

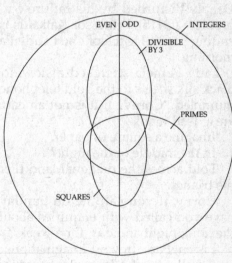

I have made an empty Venn diagram here, and the puzzle is to fit the integers 0 to 30 into their right places.

For instance, you have to put the 7 where it falls into all the right spaces, that for primes, that for odd numbers, and of course that for integers.

Answer 131

WT   Y U,T   U T   T T Y   T   T

Q132. The tragedy of scholarship?

I have nourished myself on literature but try as I may I have failed really to understand. I have lived all my life in books, devouring them eagerly, yet somehow I seem to be no wiser.

Who am I? What am I? Help me in my despair!

Answer 142

Q133. Early imagination

Deeply disturbed by his failure on Lady Pamela's imagination problem (Q115), Professor Kalkalus had been secretly folding and cutting paper. He telephoned Lady Pam at ten o'clock one Sunday morning.

Lady Pamela stretched a slow, lovely arm from beneath her black silk sheets to the gold telephone. A dark-brown sleepy voice mumbled, 'Corny? If it is not an earthquake or a revolution, you are a dead man!'

'Imagine a square of paper.'

'In the middle of the night?'

'Fold across the diagonal, and then diagonally again, dividing the triangle.'

'Corny, if you call me on Sunday before noon again, I shall have you called with enquiries about your health every hour on the hour, night and day, for a week.'

'Listen, Pam. In your imagination, cut off both sharp corners.'

'I shall cut off a least five of your limbs if I ever have the bad luck to see you again.'

'Describe the shapes you obtain from imagination only.'

Using three improper words in each sentence, Lady Pamela described some shapes. 'Now get off the – expletive – phone,' she finished.

'You cheated! I heard the scissors,' cried the Professor in real dismay. But she had rung off.

This is the folding which he described.

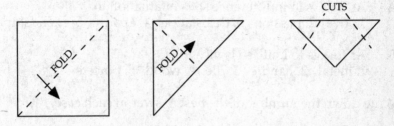

Using only your imagination, can you now describe the shapes obtained. Or you may draw your solution here.

Your answer

Answer 153

| WT | Y | US,T | U | T S | STR | T | Y | STR S | RT |

Q134. Relationships

Here is another test of judging relationships.

A.   As hate is to indifference so is infatuation to:
     1. love   2. passion   3. detestation   4. apathy   5. friendship

B.   As fork is to knife so is vice to:
     1. metal   2. handle   3. file   4. wood   5. pincers

Write down the number of the best answer in each case.

Answer 164

Q135. Straight from the horse's mouth

Maybe I was daydreaming or delusional, but I swear a race-horse spoke to me. My racing owner host was very busy with a crisis on the telephone and suggested that I might like to look at the stables by myself. I had passed a few stalls when my eye was caught by a splendid snow-white mare. I stopped and said to myself, 'A fine beast.'

The mare said, almost coyly, in a sort of neigh you could just understand, 'I bet you say that to all the mares.' When she saw my shock she apologised. 'Sorry to startle you. Not many of us that can talk let humans know that we can; but you seemed so nice, it just came out.'

'You gave me a shock,' I said.

'Shocked that a mere animal can do what human foals of three can do? That's speciesism,' she neighed, 'not a compliment like your first remark. Tell me more about what a fine animal I am.'

'You are the most beautiful milk-white horse I have ever seen,' I told the vain animal, 'and you are certainly the most intelligent.'

'That is much better. Go on, go on!'

'Did you know you are famous? There's a whisky named after you.'

The mare tossed her rich, well-groomed mane and neighed a sneering, loud laugh. 'A whisky called Rum Punch?' she neighed.

Horses are classified in many ways and go under many names. I grant you the alternate letters, but can you fill in the missing letters to complete the following list of equine names?

. H . R .

. E . D . N .

. A . F . E .

. T . L . I . N

. H . R . E .

. T . E .

. I . L .

. O . T .

. O .

. A .

Answer 175

WITH   Y F US, TH UGHT S STR T GY F ST R S RT

Q136. Connections yet again

What word connects a taunt to a non-combatant, ungenerous self-enrichment, a way of using a maritime propellant, and the insignia of a titled architectural critic?

Answer 113

Q137. How long to find our how long?

In 1934 we were digging out for house foundations. Georgie and I knew how fast we could work, and we knew how fast Jim, the genuine labourer, could work. He could knock out a complete foundation in three hours flat. Georgie, who was a tough six-footer, could do it in four hours, whereas I – a tubby shorty and lazy – with the best will in the world could not manage it in less than five hours.

We came to the last foundation on that site and decided to work on it together. All would have gone well if I had not begun to calculate. Because of the arguments and calculations about how long it should take us, it actually took four and a half hours. That is the worst thing about intellectuals on labouring jobs – they think too much.

The question is: how much time did we waste, and how long would it have taken us to complete the job without arguing, calculating and obstructing each other?

Answer 150

Q138. Sorting and ranking

Here is an untoward dog's dinner of elements from the micro-cosm and the macrocosm. The puzzle is not only to separate the microcosmic from the macrocosmic (or astronomic), but at the same time to put both sets into rank order, from small to large.

Here is the mixed up list:

1. atom 2. molecule 3. meteorite 4. star 5. crystal 6. planet 7. galaxy 8. quark 9. universe 10. electron 11. meteor

Write the names (or numbers) in their correct ascending order against the appropriate heading:

Microcosm

Macrocosm

Answer 118

Q139. Spotting the right spots

James Riddell was mightily pleased with himself for solving Kwizzer's new style of puzzle and set to work to compose them himself with elaborations. He worked hard at it, arranging dis-tractors and deceptions. Finally he faxed a completed puzzle to Kurt Kwizzer with this message.

'Dr K. Kwizzer. If you wish to have any chance of maintaining your pretensions to superiority, you will fax me this spot-locating puzzle back with the other spots correctly located and marked within one hour. Riddell.'

WITH MA Y F US, TH UGHT S A STRAT GY F AST R S RT

This is the puzzle that accompanied the message:

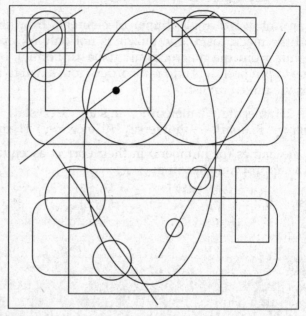

The fax came back with two more spots marked within 20 minutes and an accompanying message,

'Riddell. This sort of puzzle was my idea. Imitation is flattery, if it is good imitation. It took me ten minutes and was so stupidly obvious. Kwizzer.'

James Riddell was delighted. Can you guess why?

Look at the marked spot and mark the places in the diagram where, according to environment and logic, the other spots should go.

Answer 129

Q140. Dolly and Dirty

Dolly was a lady and Dirty was a very old Cockney. They were fast friends. Dolly drank herself stupid every night, but before she collapsed she kept all the ladies and gentlemen in the cardboard city underneath the arches amused with her tales of her prosperous childhood.

Dirty was so fond and protective of Dolly that he swore he would have a bath one of these days. He looked after her boxes, bags, bottles and other bits and pieces when she was flat out. With that lot under the arches should would have been cleaned out every night if it wasn't for him. They shared the money she begged and what an old lady in grey brought her every week.

His responsibility was cigarettes. If he had been able to count he would have known that he had accumulated a hoard of 3456 cigarette ends. But he had bronchitis and it was too cold for him to go collecting, and he was worried about how long the hoard would last.

He had discovered from experience that six cigarette ends could be re-rolled into a nice cocktail-flavoured cigarette. But would his stock last until the cold snap was over? Between them the two friends rationed themselves to 98 cigarettes a day, and he would not be able to go searching again for a week.

Dolly counted the precious hoard and said that they did not have enough for a week, but she was drunk. Next day she re-calculated when she was sober and said that they would be OK.

Was she right drunk or sober? How many cigarettes could be made from Dirty's precious hoard?

Answer 104

WITH MANY OF US, THOUGHT IS A STRATEGY OF LAST RESORT

Q141. The Professor's revenge

Professor Kalkalus had been folding and cutting paper squares in readiness for a suitable opportunity. He tackled Lady Pamela one day as they were out walking.

'I have to admit you took me by surprise with your visual imagination test when we were out riding. When I got home I solved it without using paper and scissors, but I don't expect you to believe me.'

'But I do believe you, my dear man. I would lie about such a thing but I do not think that you would.'

'You made a point; it took me a solid hour before I was sure. Then I checked and confirmed my answer.'

'What was it?'

'You mean you did not know yourself?'

'How little you know me! I had no idea.'

'Right! So now it is my turn to test you.'

He took a piece of paper from his pocket and showed it to her.

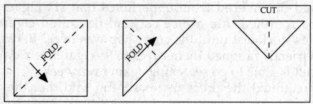

'Now use your imagination,' he said.' If you fold and cut as shown, what will you get when you unfold the cut paper?'

'My imagination is not that sort,' was all she said.

But how about your imagination? Can you solve the puzzle without trying it out with paper and scissors?

You can answer by description, or by drawing your answer in this box.

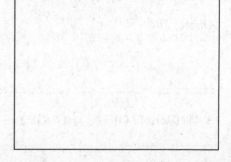

Answer 141

Q142. Square of words

This is a word square. It has the same five words down and across. Here is a clue to the five words.

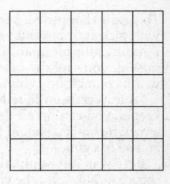

'Sheila was distraught. She wept with her friend Sue saying, 'I tried to look 'first word' but my hand slipped with the scissors and I cut off a 'fifth word' and wrecked my coiffure. What with the pain in my decayed 'second word', and the fact that my 'fourth word' are well overdue, I only wish I was 'third word' and could fly away from it all.'

Now can you fill in the word square?

Answer 152

Q143. Antique puzzles revived

Here is an example of a whole class of 'what is the difference' riddles:

What is the difference between a teacher and an engine driver?
Answer: One trains the mind and the other minds the train.

Now try this: 'What is the difference between an absent husband and a friendly lodger?'

Answer 163

A   A S O N   A O N   OO S
        O O S   ON

Q144. Finding a suitable position

This really happened. Bert Timmins had been a labourer, working with pick and shovel for many years. He was good at that job and a happy, simple man. But when the foreman retired Jock, a mischievous fellow labourer, began to stir up the poisonous worm of ambition in him.

'You have been here longest,' he said. 'You are a good time-keeper, you can do all the jobs and shift more soil in a day than any of them. You should have the job of foreman now that old so-and-so has gone.'

Bert was not sophisticated, but he had a good idea of his capacity. 'No, Jock,' he cried. 'I'd not be up to it. I'm happy as I am.'

But in the way of workmates the cruel leg-pull went on, with all the rest of the gang joining in. Finally and reluctantly Bert was persuaded to approach the site manager who, sadly, was in on the 'joke'.

Bert walked into the manager's office and blurted out, 'The chaps think I should be foreman, so I want the job.'

The manager put on a judicial look. 'It's a lot of responsibility. Do you think you are up to it?'

'Yes, boss. I can do it as well as any of 'em.'

'Could you write out the orders for tools and transport?'

There was a doubtful, defiant ring about Bert's reply. 'Yes, I certainly could. I've got a biro somewhere.'

Outside the manager's office there was a crowd of eager eavesdroppers.

The manager looked stern. 'Can you read and write?'

'As well as any of 'em, but I ain't no scholar.'

'Well, spell hammer.'

'I can spell that.'

'Well, go on then!'

Bert paused and tentatively ventured, 'H?'

Well, yes,' responded the manager.

'Er – er, is it A?'

'OK so far.'

'I go for an M next?'

'Go on! You are doing all right.'
There was a long pause.
The manager said, 'Go on, go on!'
'It's an E, isn't it?'
'Back on the shovel, Bert.'

Bert was relieved rather than disappointed. Ever after he loudly proclaimed that he would have been foreman except for one letter.

Bert was seeking a suitable position, and probably found one.

In this puzzle there is a black spot in a certain environment.

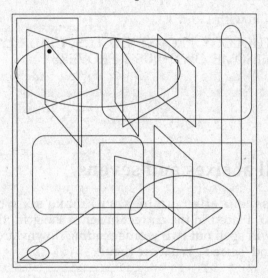

There are two other places where, logically, a similarly placed spot may be. Mark them on the drawing.

Answer 174

APP A STOP N P   A   O T NT   TOO S
O O ST   T ON

Q145. Shrimpoas 3

Here is some more mayhem with wise words for you to rectify. Can you restore these nonsense passages to their immortal proper form, and sort out the text from author or source?

There are three scrambled aphorisms, but in order to test you to the limit I have mixed the middle one in with the other two.

1. LOVE SCHOPENHAUER WHO SOLITUDE DOES NOT FREEDOM ENJOY THAN BETTER WILL NOT QUARRELLING

2. Is mixed in with 1 and 3.

3. ITS PATHOLOGY PROUST EACH SOCIAL CLASS HAS BE LONESOME OWN IRISH PROVERB

Answer 109

Q146 All at sixes and sevens

These six seven-letter jumbles will make six words when unscrambled. Placed in the correct order in the grid, the first and last letters will spell out two words reading downwards meaning 'talkative' and 'scared'. What are they?

AEIRTVY
AACEEHR
AACDOOV
ABFHSLU
ACJKLOW
AACDILR

Answer 146

Q147. How much science do you know?

There is a lot of complaint about how little knowledge of science we have in Britain.

Here is a difficult test to see how much you understand of at least the meaning of scientific words.

Listed below are 12 scientific terms and 12 definitions, but the definitions are mixed up. Write the correct letter in front of each definition in the arrowed column.

a.	an ohm	the S.I. unit of electrical capacitance
b.	epistemology	the science of the universe
c.	a sigmoid curve	a gaussian, or bell, curve
d.	palaeontology	the science and study of insects
e.	entomology	the science and study of fossils
f.	a genome	major biological taxonomy division
g.	a phylum	the support upon which a lever operates
h.	a fulcrum	an end-supported horizontal structure
i.	a cantilever	the full set of genes in a cell
j.	a normal curve	the general science of knowledge
k.	cosmology	an 'S'-shaped curve in mathematics
l.	a farad	the measure of electrical resistance

Answer 117

APP ALS TO PR NC PL AR O T N T   TOOLS
O O STR CT ON

Q148. Logical triangles

The same logic applies to all these triangles. What number should take the place of the question mark?

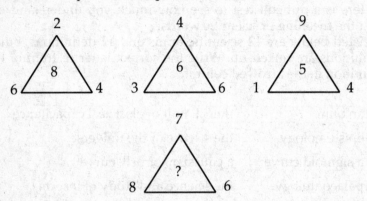

Answer 128

Q149. Crossword jigsaw

My grand-daughter was busy with forbidden scissors in my study.

'What are you doing, child?' I enquired.

'Helping you with your puzzles, Grandad.'

'Good girl! What is that you have cut up?'

'It is your crossword puzzle.'

'That's not very helpful.'

'But it is!'

'How do you mean?'

'You do very difficult puzzles, don't you, Grandad?'

'Yes, but . . .'

She interrupted, displaying the scattered pieces of the puzzle. 'This helps you to make the puzzle more difficult, doesn't it, Grandad?'

Accepting the five-year old's innovation, I set you her puzzle. So here are the dismembered pieces of the crossword. Can you do anything with them?

The blank grid may be some help.

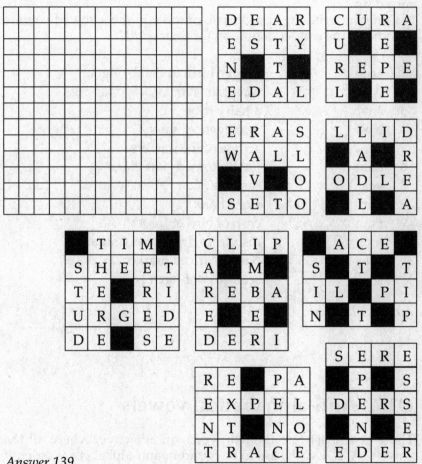

Answer 139

APP ALS TO PRINCIPL AR OFT N TH TOOLS
OF O STR CTION

Q150. Some four-letter words

Here are some less well-known, but perfectly proper, four-letter words and some definitions. The latter have, however, all been mixed up.

Can you write the appropriate number in the arrowed column to indicate the correct definition for each word?

1.	aeon		to give birth to (lamb or goat)
2.	Ainu		Egyptian symbol, key-like cross
3.	ankh		a hairy tribe
4.	brae		intelligence, 'savvy'
5.	craw		an age of the universe
6.	dahl		flat bottomed skiff (boat)
7.	yean		castrate
8.	dory		steep bank
9.	nous		crop of bird or insect
10.	loon		dish from dried peas (Indian)
11.	spay		North African market
12.	souk		scamp, boor (arch.)

Answer 105

Q151. Anti-alphabetical vowels

There is at least one English word, an adjective, where all the vowels (A, E, I, O, U) are to be found in anti-alphabetical order. If you can figure it out, my opinion of you will be the reverse of what the word means.

Answer 151

Q152. Not on the square

You have to find five words to fill up this magic word square, the same five words across and down. I have numbered the words from 1 to 5 (left to right/top to bottom). The clues to them are contained in the following paragraph.

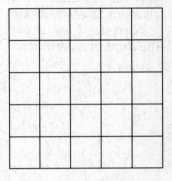

The man looks clean and neat but very poor; he is no more than a (1). But he has a sort of (2) eye for those aging widows whose sympathy and desire to care for someone he (5) on. He declares, 'I (3) you' and offers to (4) them. Then he robs them and leaves them.

Answer 162

Q153. English through darts

English is what the kids needed to learn; they were way behind. But English is what the kids hated, whether from bad home training, bad teaching or whatever.

Mr Simon Tooter, the teacher, was in despair. He loved English and could not understand those who did not. He asked the class what they were keen on.

Influenced by a current TV craze, twenty-three pupils shouted out with one voice, 'Darts!' Mr Tooter shrugged in despair. But Joe Cleaver, his one clever boy and often his biggest problem, spoke up.

'What about a darts game that teaches English, then?'

APPEALS TO PRINCIPLE ARE OFTEN THE TOOLS
OF OBSTRUCTION

'You come up with some daft ideas, Cleaver, but that tops them all,' said his teacher with a soft sigh. But there was an enthusiastic clamour from the class.

Next day Cleaver came in with a piece of card like this fixed to the front of a dartboard.

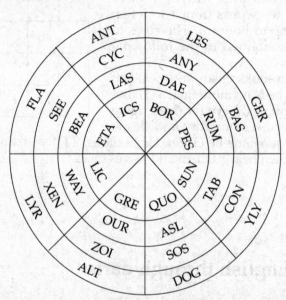

Mr Tooter sighed. 'More mischievous nonsense from you, Cleaver. Do give it a rest.' But he noticed that the whole class was in eager excitement. Keenness – he had never seen it before.

Joe Cleaver seemed to be taking over. 'This is the game,' he explained. 'You each have a go with two darts. If you hit two syllables that make up an English word you gain a point and keep the darts. If you fail you lose a point and pass the darts on to the next player.'

At playtime the boys wanted to stay on with the darts and had to be driven from the class. Mr Tooter had most points and Cleaver was next, largely due to bad throwing. Mr Tooter looked happy for the first time that term.

Can you list all sixteen re-assembled words?

Answer 173

160

Q154. Riddle-me-ree

Still reviving antique riddles, I dare you to try this:

> He went into the woods and caught it.
> Then he sat down and sought it.
> Because he could not find it,
> Home with him he brought it.

How do you make sense of that?

Answer 108

Q155. Air combat tennis

Opposing fighter planes (A and B) were speeding towards each other, each travelling at 800 mph in windless conditions. When they were exactly 500 miles apart, plane A launched a target-seeking missile at plane B at 2000 mph. When the missile reached the target area the sophisticated electronics on plane B turned the missile round and directed it back at plane A. But plane A had the same technology and returned the missile towards plane B.

The projectile's flight continued backwards and forwards in this way until the two planes collided head-on at the same time as the missile exploded, causing a rain of fine metal fragments.

Ignoring the turning time, how many miles did the missile travel before that disastrous conclusion?

Answer 157

I I		GH H	G	I	, H	I
		HI GI		I	LL	

Q156. Further connections

Can you work out these obscure connections? What is the linking idea and what are the references?

What connects a tourist attraction just north of Buffalo; a period of foliage discolouration stateside; a follower of immodesty; and the result of an atomic chain reaction?

Answer 116

Q157. Wonky weighing

I was buying a big sapele log by weight in a remote spot in a tropical forest. I noticed that the primitive scales, rigged up from timbers, were a bit rough and ready. I took a few measurements and found out that the situation was as shown below.

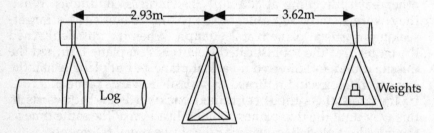

The forester asked me to pay for 9.33 tonnes on the basis of the weight that counterbalanced the log. I was up against it for time and had to work out what the bias was. I had a slide rule and after an argument I got my figure accepted.

What was it?

Answer 127

Q158. Mental paperwork

Such a simple set of foldings and cuttings, and such variable results! Perhaps you are getting used to them and may be able to tackle this one.

It is all in the mind! Start with a fanciful square of paper, find you fantasy scissors, and start work.

Fold to the right across the square, then downward at right angles and finally upwards diagonally. Now cut a rectangular nick from the middle of the long surface (see illustration).

Draw or describe the resulting paper scraps when unfolded. How many pieces are there, and what shape?

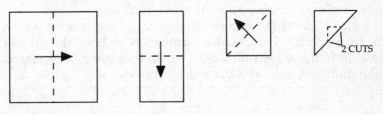

Answer 138

Q159. The aliens in doubt

The alien invaders from the space ship colony, having selected the most capable and intelligent human beings, are beginning to use them rather than the robots they brought with them which are prone to break down in Earth conditions. Well selected and well treated people might be less intelligent than the robots, but they were more reliable and there was no manufacture cost.

| I I NO | NO GH O H | | GOO | MIN | , H M IN |
| | HING I | O | I | LL | |

Most remaining adults had survived multiple tests and, of course, they were getting used to them and coaching each other to pass them, even though this was strictly forbidden. The selected humans had to work hard and be obedient but they were getting the measure of their more intelligent masters and beginning to exploit them, as a dog learns to exploit its master. One way to do this was to create games for the aliens' amusement.

The humans never saw their alien masters. All communications came over computer channels, and all attempts to locate the source of the signals failed, and the perpetrators were punished.

Kurt Kwizzer was one of the survivors and he had become Quizmaster and Clown. The aliens were delighted when he found a puzzle that they could not instantly solve and rewarded him with smoked salmon and vodka, of which he was fond.

Here is one of the puzzles that brought him such a reward. In the overlapping figures some numbers have been shown and you have to find the logical rule by which they have been placed and what numbers should replace the dots.

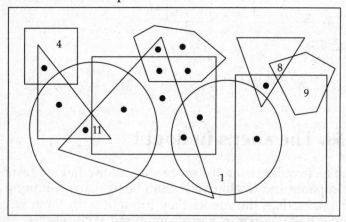

When he sent this via his computer screen to his normal contact he did not get back the usual immediate correct response. Instead, delight of delights, they asked for more information! He inserted a few more numbers, and they managed to solve it.

Can you replace all the dots with the correct numbers?

Answer 149

Q160. Ask a silly question . . .

Harold Farquarson and Cecil Beaufort were busy. Their aim was malevolent. They wanted to take advantage of Dr Surd, the new mathematics master who had displeased them. Currying favour with the less advanced boys, the silly novitiate had taken to finding ways to put them down in class. 'It is presumptuous, Beaufort, to be working on problems in calculus when, as I see here, you have made an absurd mistake in simple addition.' That sort of thing.

They worked out a simple question which was posed so as to look difficult.

'Can you help us, Sir? My father, Sir Quentin, will not tell us the weight of the medicine ball we work with. He set it as a riddle and says that I am a fool and the school is no good because we cannot solve it.'

Concerned at the possible threat to his own reputation, Dr Surd said, 'Tell me the riddle; I feel sure I can help with it if it is beyond you.'

'Well, Sir, he says the ball weighs 100lbs divided by half its real weight.'

Dr Surd thought for a moment, looked embarrassed, and then said, 'That is a ridiculous, meaningless riddle, not a mathematical problem. We are here to learn how to solve serious problems.'

There was a suppressed titter in the class. During the rest of the lesson he set the boys problems, and while they worked on them he could be seen scribbling on his scrap pad.

At the end of the lesson Harold put his hand up. 'I know it's a silly problem,' he said, 'but Harold and I came up with an answer and we would like your expert opinion on it.'

What answer to this problem can you come up with?

Answer 106

> IT I NOT NO GH TO HA   A GOO MIN , TH MAIN
>   THING I TO   IT   LL

Q161. In similar circumstances

Polly Titian was arguing with the press gang. Now that she was a Minister she was on the defensive. The *Sunday Squawk* man especially kept pressing her about one of those cases where hardship had arisen because someone fell between the definitions of the bureaucrats' regulations.

'Every case is unique,' she argued, 'yet we have to write the regulations as though all cases fell neatly into one of the defined categories.'

'But this is an obvious case of injustice,' squawked the *Squawk* man. 'The regulations should take account of it.'

Polly began to shout. 'The number of possible circumstances is infinite, but the regulations have to finish with a finite number of categories. It is impossible for the legislator to think of everything, but you in the press gang make a national scandal out of every rare case that slips between the rules.'

Then she showed them this diagram that one of her officials had drawn.

'Let me set you a problem,' Polly said to the journalists. 'Here is a case: there is a spot marking a case in particular circumstances.' She pointed to the black spot in the diagram. 'However, there are several other places in the diagram where the same circumstances apply, although different in detail. Can you find them? That is what you expect us to do.'

Can you mark where the other spots should be placed? They must be in the same environmental circumstances as the existing spot. How many more spots should there be?

Answer161

Q162. Simple addition?

One of the tests set by the robots on behalf of the hyper-intelligent extra-terrestrial aliens was the simple one of comprehending their system of numeration. Millions of people were eliminated at this hurdle.

Here is the simple addition sum in their numerals which caused so much human destruction. Can you do it, or would you have gone under?

Answer 172

IT IS NOT NOUGH TO HA   A GOO   MIN , TH MAIN
THING IS TO US IT   LL

Q163. More imaginary folding & cutting

Professor Kalkalus had tried the imaginary paper folding and cutting idea on his students at an evening class in applied mathematics. He had been delighted to find that all but one of the students failed. Her name was Caroline Penser. She got the first right immediately, but said she could not do the second. The Professor wanted to test her further, so he gave her and the rest of the class this one – a new development.

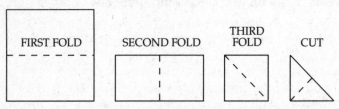

He drew this upon the blackboard, and explained it in these terms. 'Take a square of paper, mentally fold it downwards in half, then right in half, then diagonally downwards again in half. In your imagination bisect the triangle across the hypotenuse. Draw or describe the result when unfolded.

'I wonder if anyone can solve it out of their head?'

He had to stop a couple of students from surreptitiously cutting paper under their desk. Caroline was silent a long time, then shouted and cried out 'Eureka! I've got it.'

'Show us on the board, Caroline.'

She went out to the front, and drew on the board swiftly and surely.

The Professor was impressed. 'Near enough, Caroline!'

Without folding paper or using scissors, can you show what she drew on the board or describe it.

Answer135

Q164. The aliens falter

Under the rule of the ET aliens, after the first period of complete domination, cautious human alliances began to form. Kurt Kwizzer and James Riddell became collaborators, if not friends. Most of the robots had broken down under earth conditions, and human solidarity against the aliens was strengthening, so that no-one seemed to be able to repair them.

The secret task of the puzzle-master pair was to find puzzles that the aliens failed to solve, and this to undermine their morale. Working on a growing knowledge of the mental weak points of the aliens, deprived of the robots to do their thinking for them, they devised specially designed teasers. Ermyntrude Eunous, Caroline Penser, Professor Kalkalus and Lady Pamela Swot were all in touch via the computer network, helping in this task.

This, oddly enough, is one of the first puzzles that, because of a weakness of imagination, defeated the aliens.

```
  .   .   .   .   .

  .   .   .   .   .

  .   .   .   .   .

  .   .   .   .   .

  .   .   .   .   .
```

You are to imagine every square that can be drawn on this grid, with the sole condition that every vertex, or corner, of each square must fall on one of the 25 dots.

How many different squares meet this simple condition?

Answer 168

IT IS NOT ENOUGH TO HAVE A GOOD MIND, THE MAIN
THING IS TO USE IT WELL

Q165. Even more connections

How are these related? Scrofula; a big, striped predator; a high ranking bibulous lover of music; and a fictional monstrous simian.

What word unites these ideas?

Answer 115

Q166. A ten-word square

This is an unusual word square because the across words are different from the down words. The words have been numbered, and the clues to them are contained in the following tale.

	6	7	8	9	10
1					
2					
3					
4					
5					

Lord Jasper Gaunt, whenever he could, would (1) after any attractive (2). Unwillingly, the victim would often submit to His Lordship and allow him to become her (7). The evil man thought it (5) when, as often happened, the poor creature became (3) in shape and a (9) event followed. One day this happened with a woman so perfectly formed that she would have been called an (8) if she were a butterfly. But she had a young, jealous lover and despite the Baron's (4) connections, the distraught young man put Lord Jasper to the (6), made an end of him and was duly hanged. The grieving victim cut her wrists and died on his prison grave, even as his very (10) was sounding.

Answer 126

Q167. Numberless assignation

Lady Pamela rang the Professor at a time when he was deeply into a difficult problem for the atomic physicists.

'There's a barbecue,' she said. 'You really must come right away.' She was in a perverse and playful mood and the Professor knew what that meant.

'A barbecue, in winter with snow on the ground?' he asked.

'We have an open fire at the house I've borrowed.'

'An indoor barbecue! How many will be there?'

'My guests are my business.'

'I don't want names, just a number.'

'Two, darling. Just big, strong you and meek little me. Oh, and some dead animals, steaks and sausages, and fermented fruit juices, and stuff.'

There was no doubt the Professor was attracted. Neither was there any doubt that Lady Pam would take it very ill if he did not go.

'OK,' he said. 'What is the address?'

'Kensington Park Road, my sweet love.'

'What number, dear?'

'Do you really want to come?'

'I said so.'

'But can you prove it? If you really want to come you will solve this puzzle.'

'Oh, no! Not that childish business again.'

'Do you want to come, or not?'

'OK. What is the puzzle?'

'It is the house number. If it is a multiple of 3, it is between 50 and 59. If it is not a multiple of 4, then it is between 60 and 69. If it is not a multiple of 6, then it is between 70 and 79.

'Now if you really love me you will turn up within the hour to the most beautifully sanglant-flared tender Sirloin steak you ever tasted, with that burgundy – La Tache or whatever – that you like and, as a tinsy extra, my fond affection.'

At what number did the Professor turn up?

Answer 137

Q168. Many 'ands make light work

The porter was asked by Sir Quentin Beaufort for the times of the next few trains to London.

'The man is mad,' he said to his son when he heard the reply.

'What did he say, Father?'

'He just started tooting like a bugle.'

'So his son, Cecil, asked and got the reply.

'Two to two; two; two two, too.'

He translated the seven 'toots' for his father, and they caught the 2.02.

Legitimate sentences with the same word repeated numerous times are fun. Can you contrive a proper sentence with five consecutive 'and's?

Answer 148

Q169. Another head transplant job

RING	LIFT
SACK	TACT
BED	PEEL
OF	ACE
SAIL	DOTE
FOOD	TRIP

You have to transplant the heads – the first letters of each word – replacing them with the same six letter word reading downwards, so that you are left with twelve still good English words.

What word will do this?

Answer 159

Q170. Can you count?

Here is a simple question. How many circles and how many rectangles are there in this diagram?

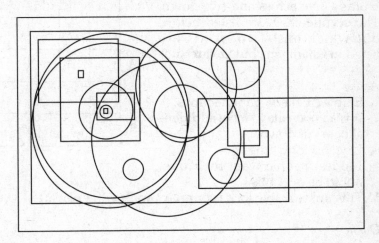

Answer 107

Q171. Still connections

There is a word that brings all these to mind: affecting affection for an instrument of chastisement; a greeting under a parasitic growth; an old way to swear legally; announcing evidence of affection. What is the word?

Answer 171

T E E EOF E N E E OFTEN	
E ENT O E O N O	

Q172. Cryptic clued ten-word square

This a word square, but it has ten words – five across and five down. The cryptic clues are listed below, but watch out! Two words are listed in Chambers, but are archaic.

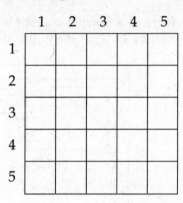

Across
1. Ship's crockery, imperfections.
2. It is a good rule to have additional beer cut down.
3. Lately, a long time ago.
4. Modest people want their due, not to be over this.
5. This unbreakable lock is burglar proof, self replacing.

Down
1. Good looking, intelligent but what a pain.
2. You are up at all hours when you get to these districts.
3. Tell the crowd, this is not zero 4-across.
4. It's ages since Scots had such small servings.
5. Sliders, preceded in craft.

Answer 120

Q173. Related domino triplets

On the following page are two sets of dominoes (A & B) that are related in some way. Below them is a third set (C) and four alternative sets (D-G) with which it can be related. Which of the four should be paired with C so as to have the same relationship as A and B have with each other?

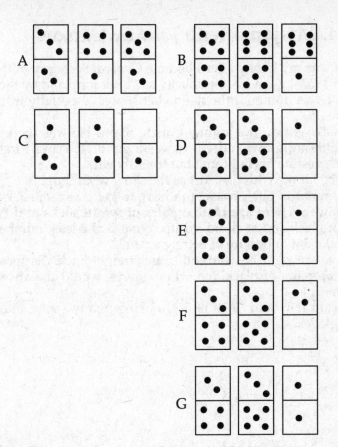

A   B

C   D

E

F

G

Answer 130

T E DES E OF   E   N C E E OFTEN
E ENTS O   BECO N SO

Q174. My joust with Johnny Carson

Mensa was my hobby after I became General Secretary of the tiny club in 1952. I got a lot of publicity as I built it up and by the early sixties I was doing all the main chat shows, especially in Britain and the USA.

I finally got on the Johnny Carson Show. He was the big boy then, although now retired. It was a good chat and I held my ground, despite his lightning but friendly wit.

But he hit me with this, just as the show wound up.

'The room is pitch black. You have to get a pair of socks from the drawer. There are twelve pairs of white socks and twelve pairs of black socks, all mixed up. What is the least number you must take out to be sure of getting a pair?'

I gave the right answer and came straight back. 'Supposing it had been pairs of black and white gloves, would the answer be the same?'

He said it would. Was he right? How many socks, and how many gloves?

Answer 114

Q175. Numerical relations

$$X = 1375682 \qquad Y = 3976842$$

X is to Y as Z is to which of the following:

$$Z = 8647341$$

$$A = 3890211$$
$$B = 2548579$$
$$C = 2048765$$
$$D = 9867345$$

Answer 125

Q176. I tangle with the Barracuda

I have forgotten his name, but one chat show host in Toronto was know as the Barracuda because he had a reputation for eating his guests alive. My Mensa friends said he would destroy me and leave me silent and weeping in front of millions.

Nevertheless, trembling with nerves I turned up at the TV studio. The interview was a doddle, with a faintly nasty question about elitism for which I chose from six funny stock answers. At the end I invited him to apply to join Mensa and he said he would.

In the dressing room later, Win – my wife – was saying, 'There you are, it was not so bad. You handled him OK.' Then through the thin partition to the Barracuda's dressing room we heard his wife say to him, 'There, you see, it was not so bad. You handled him OK.' My reputation from the Carson Show had stood me in good stead. He had given me a gentle ride.

The one puzzle he tried on me was this. It is one of those where any expert knows the answer. Most users of firearms will find it no challenge, but even some of them fail it.

Solve this from first principles. It is tricky! You are a good shot and have a rifle which consistently hits to the left of where you aim. Which of these alternative actions should you take?

A. Move the front sight to the left.
B. Move the back sight to the left.
C. Move the front sight to the right.
D. Move the back sight to the right.

Answer 136

THE DES RE OF   E R N CLE ER OFTEN
RE ENTS O R BECO   N SO

177

Q177. Absurdly meticulous pouring

Kurt Kwizzer, James Riddell, Lady Pamela Swot and Professor Cornelius Kalkalus were sharing a prison cell. They had been arrested by one of the few remaining groups of human soldiers who were loyal to the aliens. The soldiers had been instructed to guard their prisoners until the aliens decided what action to take to suppress their subversive activities.

Lady Pamela and the Professor got to work on the soldiers. They soon succeeded in filling them with doubts about what they had done, but not in obtaining their release. The soldiers chose what seemed to them the safest course and decamped, leaving the four prisoners with a supply of food. This took the form of an all-purpose nourishing fluid, stored in some jugs.

Not realising the soldiers had gone, the four prisoners began to amuse each other with word games and riddles. After a while the Professor began to consider their distribution problem. How were they to divide their rations fairly?

They had four jugs: an empty 2 litre one, 5 litre and 7 litre full jugs, and an empty 12 litre jug. That was all! 'What,' the Professor asked the others, 'is the minimum number of pourings required to get the 12 litres accurately divided into four equal amounts?'

The two quiz kings took on this problem while Lady Pam used a nail-file to prise out a loose brick. She used it to bang loudly on the iron door of their cell while the Professor shouted loudly, 'Help! Let us out!' in several languages with monotonous persistence.

After two hours, working amidst all that clamour, Riddell and Quizzer compared their calculations. They found that Riddell had a plan with three less pourings than his colleague. He contained his triumph and Quizzer contained his chagrin while they set about the task of dividing up the liquid food into the four jugs.

But before they had a chance to start drinking it, the banging and shouting finally attracted the attention of some local workmen who set them free.

What was the successful pouring plan? How many pourings?

Answer 147

Q178. More spot spotting!

Seeing complex relationships is difficult, but rewarding if you can do it.

I have marked a spot in this confused diagram which has its own special environmental relationships. You have to find out whether there are any other spots which are similarly related to the figures around them.

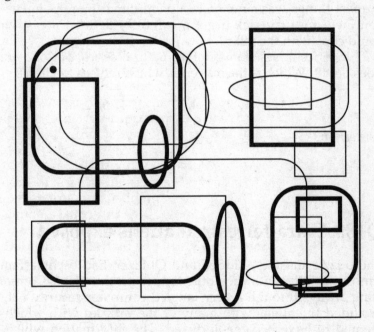

Can you find any other spots? How many are there? They must be in the same circumstances as the dot that is already marked.

Answer 158

THE DES RE OF   PPE R NG CLE ER OFTEN
PRE ENTS O R BECO   NG SO

179

Q179. Which is the odd one out?

I was often the odd one out in my early life. I was unpredictable, a maverick. I always wanted to think it out for myself rather than follow the precedent or the crowd.

It is a policy that only rarely pays off. It may be alright to have a few odd-balls like that, but civilised life would be impossible if we were all rampant individualists. I learned later that conformity in most things was simpler, less painful and more popular – so I confined my maverick urge to carefully defined areas where I could cope with the risks.

This series arises from another natural series, but one number does not fit. Which is the maverick which refuses to 'fit in'?

$$1, 1, 1, 2, 2, 4, 2, 4, 2, 4, 6, 2, 4$$

Answer 169

Q180. Extra-terrestrial aliens exposed

The puzzle masters, Riddell and Quizzer, had become familiar, almost friendly, with each other and with the aliens. Communicating always through a very tangled computer security net, they provided the aliens with many of the puzzles with which they seemed to have become addicted. The information which they were gaining from these contacts was being processed by Professor Kalkalus, who led a large investigating team assembled by the now powerful Human Underground Government.

There were still some countries and groups repairing robots for the aliens, but all their own repair facilities had broken down or been sabotaged by the human underground. Without their robots the aliens, hidden deep in the complexity of the world's communications network, had no executive arm and no power except over those who had the habit of obedience to them. They still had some strategic level power, but more and more governments and organisations were functioning normally again as far as they could having regard to the great decrease in population.

The one remaining and ridiculous mystery was the location of the aliens. Computer experts and hackers had gone over the networks every way, but they simply could not locate the source of the signals – the centre. The signals from the aliens seemed to come from every direction. The aliens provided the humans with codes which they constantly changed and somehow picked them up out of the vast world communications and computer network.

Then came a new development. The puzzling ubiquity of the signals was penetrated. The system was shown by the Professor's team to be hierarchic. There was a vaguely local source around the London area from which very minute signals came which somehow triggered those that came from everywhere throughout the network.

One of the Professor's sub-teams, led by Ermyntrude Eunous who was now nineteen years old, went a step further and found an even fainter, more local source of almost imperceptible signals which triggered the previous recognised lowest hierarchic level. By very complex statistical mathematics she fixed the exact spot in a small dilapidated empty house in Putney, but the most careful examination of the house and its surroundings revealed nothing. Though her discovery was kept secret, the same suggestion began to come up again and again from other experts. However, repeated and very thorough searches all round the house and the immediate area all drew a blank.

Professor Kalkalus called a conference of senior researchers including his wife, Pamela. He summarised the situation. 'An undetectable source excites a vast number of secondary stations which we cannot find. Their collective signals are picked up everywhere and the information filters its way correctly through the network. We must be making a fundamental false assumption at some point – we are working on the wrong lines.'

THE DESIRE OF APPEARING CLEVER OFTEN
PREVENTS OUR BECOMING SO

'So what is new?', said Lady Pamela. 'You are just stating the obvious, but the best brains in the underground spend all their time on the problem and have come up with nothing.'

Ermyntrude Eunous made a contribution. 'The original signals are almost too faint to detect, except by a statistical method which takes a long time. At each of several relay stages they become more widespread and stronger. Then they are filtered into the network in such a way that location of the source is impossible.'

Lady Pamela became very still and shushed everyone who tried to say anything. 'No, no! Let me think!' Everyone stayed silent for several minutes, wondering what she would come up with. Then Pamela cried out 'Eureka! That must be it; it must be!'

She passed her idea to Cornelius and, instead of entering into a heated debate as usual, he froze with a fixed intent look. A minute later he said 'Let's check it out.'

'Now?'

'Now!'

They telephoned around and shortly afterwards, having collected the two puzzle masters and made careful preparations, Ermyntrude and the rest of the team set off for Putney. They took no weapons, but a great variety of special powders and fluids.

Lady Pamela's insight proved to be correct and as a result the aliens and their menace came to an abrupt end. Mankind was once more its own master.

Can you make any sort of guess as to what Lady Pamela's lateral thinking was? What was the 'frame of reference' error she had discovered? What was the very natural but false assumption that led everyone astray? The aliens were genuine and they had come to earth from outer space and gained power using a strange ability to penetrate the vast international computer, telephone and news network and to work on some people's minds. They had the help at first of an irresistible army of robots, now largely out of action. Why could they not be located?

Answer 180

THE ANSWERS

A1. How to move sleepers (Q11)

We jointly lifted one end of a sleeper onto an offcut block, leaving a metre or so projecting. Then Georgie stood on that end, tending to lift the other end. With the right fulcrum distance, and Georgie's counterbalancing weight, I was able to lift the other end of the sleeper and swing it round to another offcut block, a metre of two forwards.

Then I stood on my overlapping end and Georgie shifted his end to another offcut block in the same way. By arranging two parallel lines of staggered offcuts, and alternately standing on our end and then lifting and swinging it, we made fair progress.

The sight of this unorthodox labouring method caused great wonder and doubt among the professional labourers in the surrounding houses who watched us very closely. The matter was ruled out of order because we were probably just drunk, as we had been with the poles.

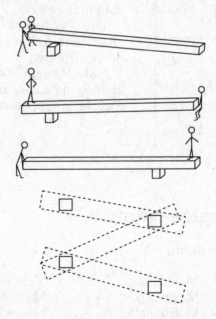

A2. Unfair square (Q20)

Lady Pamela had realised that the square could be completed using zero and negative integers, as shown opposite. Who said you may not? There is no rule against it, it is merely not usual. But no wonder she was angry that she had been slow to spot a hidden false assumption.

12	-1	-2	9
1	6	7	4
5	2	3	8
0	11	10	-3

A3. Multiplying magic squares (Q30)

32	1	128
64	16	4
2	256	8

The product of rows, columns and diagonals is 4096.

The Professor had spotted the chauffeur delivering the letter, but never admitted it.

Lady Pamela told him it had taken as long as a day because she forgot that the lowest power of two – 2^0 – is 1.

A4. Wriggle reading (Q40)

The eight words are:

Malediction
Mountaineer
Matriculate
Moneymaking

Melancholic
Marchioness
Misspelling
Metalworker

A5. Monochrome wires (Q50)

I clamped together two of the identical wires at the motor end, and labelled the other wire 'X'. Then I borrowed an umbrella and found my way with a mate through the dark labyrinth of the site to the manhole.

At the manhole, with my mate holding the umbrella over me, I tested the three wire pairs with my battery and bulb in order to find out which two were connected by my clamp. Finding the two connected ones, I could label the other one as 'X'.

I then clamped that end of the 'X' wire to one of the other two, which I labelled 'Y'. The remaining wire I labelled 'Z'.

I returned to the workshop, where I unclamped the pair of connected wires and tested all three pair combinations for continuity, as I had at the other end. This told me which wire to label 'Y' (because it was clamped to 'X') and which was 'Z'.

This diagram illustrated the process.

When we started up the ancient motor again there were two reactions. From the foreman: 'Took long enough!' and from my mates, who had been happily playing cards and drinking tea: sour looks.

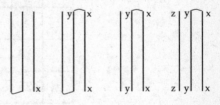

A6. Mon conversion (Q60)

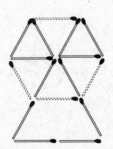

Zut! Alors! La solution! La conversion comme il faut.

A7. Change letters, make a word (Q70)

WINTER.

A8. Daftypuz (Q80)

GURU RUG.   GOLF LOG.   KOALA OK.

A9. Robust politeness (Q90)

15	19	23	7	11
27	6	10	14	18
9	13	22	26	5
21	25	4	8	17
3	12	16	20	24

A10. Can you cut free? (Q10)

If the paper is folded as illustrated and a cut made as shown, there will be nine pieces.

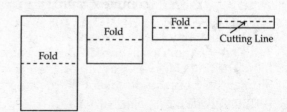

Fold

Fold

Fold

Cutting Line

A11. The quality of quality control (Q1)

Mr Poker was unjust. The bad batch could be found in fewer weighings.

Caroline was in tears as her mother berated her for losing her first job. 'But Mummy, it only needed one weighing, I am really sure.'

'Stupid girl! You were a bighead at school, but this is work. First day you think you know better than your boss. You'll never keep a job.'

Caroline's brother was more sympathetic when he came home later that evening. 'How *did* you do it, Carrie?'

'I took one grotchet from batch 1, two from batch 2, and so on up to twelve from batch 12. I weighed the whole lot and found that the total was 267.3mg too heavy. That was eleven times 24.3mg, the difference between the two types of grotchet. That meant it was batch eleven that had the heavy grotchets, because I had eleven of those on the scale.'

'Girls are not supposed to be that clever,' said her brother.

A12. Classifying (Q12)

A1 pairs with C3 and A4 pairs with C1. Each pair contains the same six items, although differently arranged.

A13. You are a contortionist – 1 (Q83)

You are are contortionist, you really are! The answer is so kickself simple. Start as described and do a complete turn, your right hand turning clockwise, until your finger tips are touching again. Stop at this point, and make it the starting position for the double turn manoeuvre.

Reverse the procedure, your right hand now turning anti-clockwise, until you are back with your hands in the prayer position, and continue to rotate your hands in the same direction until your finger tips are touching again, but with the opposite arm on top.

You have completed two complete revolutions, finger tips together at the start and coming together twice more, without parting your hands. Zut! Alors!

A14. Names can be awkward (Q74)

1D T. S. Eliot – Poet 2H Sir Karl Popper – Philosopher of Science 3C Dame Nellie Melba – Opera Singer 4A Pierre-Simon, Marquis de Laplace – Mathematical Astronomer 5E Bonar Law – British Politician 6B Sir Arthur Pinero – Playwright 7G James Clerk Maxwell – Physicist 8F Jack Hobbs – Cricketer

A15. Tell the truth (Q65)

I rang the brothers' house and, after introductions, asked 'I want to know whether to buy into Thingamy Inc. What would be your brother's advice?'

'He would advise you to buy,' I was told.

So I left it alone, and there was no takeover. I knew that whichever brother I had been speaking to, I should do the opposite. The truthful brother would have accurately reported his brother's lie, and the lying brother would have misreported his brother's truth.

Either way, what I heard was a lie.

A16. Going straight for a long way (Q56)

It is so obvious, once you know. I wish I had thought of it! The name tells you – you use a chalk-line.

Rub a cord with chalk. Rest it on the surface, setting the cord on the two required endpoints of the line. You and your mate at the other end pull very tight and wait for the cord to stop moving. Lift one end of the cord an inch or so and let go. It will fly back, leaving a long dead straight chalk line right along the surface.

You should only count this as a correct answer if you have never seen it done, but thought of it for yourself.

A17. Kid fits bits (Q47)

Ermyntrude found some of the dreadful school loo-paper which is semi-transparent. Moving the paper around she shakily traced the shapes with a pencil until she had made up the assembled square as shown below.

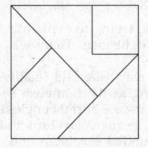

A18. Goldilocks Ermyntrude (Q38)

This is the old song that Ermyntrude deciphered in spite of the archaic words, which she decided were spelling mistakes. She loved it and was always singing it afterwards.

> Goldilocks, Goldilocks, wilt thou be mine?
> Thou shalt not wash dishes, nor yet feed the swine;
> But sit on a cushion and sew a fine seam,
> And feed upon strawberries, sugar and cream.

A19. Reading impossible drawings (Q29)

Caroline was right. The object is the intersection of two cylinders of the same diameter. This is the drawing she produced to show what the object would look like.

 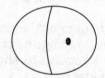

View from   View from
above   side (corner)

She took some time trying to explain it to Billy Brain and a growing circle of draughtsmen. There was an argument which embarrassed her.

'Let me put it this way,' she said finally. 'Cut a piece from a cylindrical rod as long as its diameter. Then put it in a lathe between centres, with its axis at right angles to the turning axis of the lathe. Its section is a square: just turn it until it is round. Then you will have two rounded elevations and one square one, will you not, Mr Brain?'

Then she returned to her desk and got on with her work. She

had been warned of making another exhibition of herself. The argument among the draughtsmen continued and developed until the supervisor intervened.

He scratched his head, then went away for an hour. He came back with a small turning from the workshop. He showed it to the senior draughtsmen and to Billy Brain. 'It fits,' he said. 'Who would have thought it? Now who was it who started this argument in the first place?'

No one remembered!

A20. Obstacle cricket (Q92)

T	H	R	O	W
H	E	A	V	E
R	A	V	E	L
O	V	E	R	S
W	E	L	S	H

A21. Never take the last (Q21)

There is a hierarchy of rules:

1. Never leave your opponent two of the three heaps with the same number in them.
2. If ever your opponent leaves two equal heaps, grab the whole of the third heap, leaving him the two equal heaps.
3. If your opponent takes a complete heap, leaving two unequal

heaps, take the excess from the larger heap to leave him two equal heaps.

4. Once you opponent is faced with two equal heaps, however many he takes from one heap, you take the same number from the opposite heap, until both heaps are down to 2.

5. If he then takes 1 from one heap, you take both from the other heap. If he takes both from one heap, you take 1 from the other.

I count it a good answer if you worked out this list of rules. But if you are to win consistently, especially against an opponent who has also learned the secret, you need to know the unbeatable combinations for three heaps.

Your aim is to leave one of these combinations to your opponent, and never to leave him a situation from which he can create one of these combinations for you to face. Provided you apply the above rules correctly once your opponent has been faced with one of these combinations, you must win.

Winning Combinations
1 - 1 - 1
1 - 2 - 3
1 - 4 - 5
2 - 5 - 7
3 - 4 - 7
3 - 5 - 6

A22. Mathematical flirtation (Q2)

This diagram shows how the code works.

It is based on a Fibonacci series. Each number is the sum of the previous two.

The last two – 13 and 21 – total 34, her age.

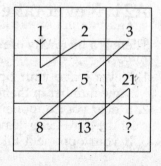

A23. Gorging sickening pastries (Q13)

Cecil called out 'better' within the time limit, explaining that the first list of words all have a double consonant with the same vowel on either side of the pair.

He was right, but as he started triumphantly to consume the prize he suddenly left the room – to be sick in the toilet. When he came back his hard-earned prize was gone, though he showed little concern at the theft.

The lesson is certainly 'Don't be too clever', but also, which is much the same, 'Moderation in all things'.

A24. You are a contortionist - 2 (Q84)

You simply fold your arms *before* you take hold of the two ends of the cord. If you then unfold them, the trick is done – the knot is tied.

A25. It can be done (Q75)

If you saw it, OK. If not, the answer is irritating.

The product of all those integers is nought. Why? Because one of them is nought. Zero is an integer, and if you multiply any number of positive integers by nought you have . . . . nought.

A26. Symbolic magic (Q66)

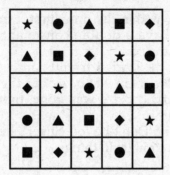

A27. Wonky wisdom (Q57)

'Every man's rights are equal but his responsibilities should be in accord with his capacity.'

A28. Leaving things (Q48)

Farouk made a habit of visiting his father on every third day. He was not always quite regular – there were accidents when he or someone in his family were ill, for example – but he kept a record, and when he missed a day or two he made extra visits to bring the sum right.

The other sons visited a lot in the first six months but then, hopeless about guessing the right number of visits, gradually fell off.

Farouk used the gold as security for a loan to set up a vineyard and melon farm using modern agricultural methods and made a great success. He was able to support his brothers when business went wrong for them.

A29. Ermyntrude squares accounts (Q39)

This is the completed word square.

L	I	M	E	S
I	N	A	N	E
M	A	N	T	A
E	N	T	E	R
S	E	A	R	S

A30. Winning when you can't play (Q93)

I never tried to hit the central marbles but, pretending even less skill than I had, I flipped my marbles a very short distance, and cursed my clumsiness. Shots from the opposite end that failed to hit a marble usually came very close to my end and were easy to pick off. If none were near enough, I could recapture my own short misses which were a long, tough shot for my opponent.

It worked like a charm. I won bags and bags of marbles and the other lads never twigged. What a little horror I was. For a few marbles!

Were you artful enough to spot my trick?

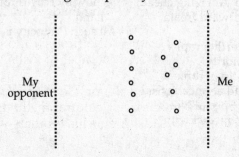

A31. Ermyntrude and the law (Q31)

Here is the verse with the rhymes restored. If you have completed the poem gradually, it will have lessened the shock of these revelations. I am sad about that.

ERMYNTRUDE AND THE LAW

The trouble with young
  Ermyntrude
Was not that she was rough or
  rude;
The problem was her attitude.
The horrid, pert, presumptuous tot
Had got to be a horrid swot
And understand an awesome lot.

What licence has a child of three
To go beyond her ABC
And read and write like you and
  me?
Her family life was just a mess,
For what endears an infant less
Than beating Dad and Mum at
  chess?

Her poor young teacher was
  upset,
When teaching her the alphabet,
To find the little demon get
To know Cyrillic, Roman, Greek
And Hebrew too. Amazing cheek,
Even in such a forward freak.

Is not advanced orthography,
Without due seniority,
Improper in a child of three?
Her worried Head at once agreed
The infant had a Special Need.
She felt compelled to act with
  speed.

She sent for a psychologist
To test, assess and thus assist
With this scholastic anarchist.
The Ed. Psych. tested her for days –
Many a time, in many ways –
Until he fell into a daze.

They found that she was testing
  him.
Resulting in the rather grim
Conclusion that the man was dim.
They tried detention and the cane
And other punishments, in vain.
It only sharpened up her brain.

They put her under freezing
  showers,
And talked to her for hours and
  hours,
And even gave her sweets and
  flowers;
But could not make her under-
stand.
So now by Law throughout the
  Land
All such Precocity is Banned.

Victor Serebriakoff

A32. Label correction (Q22)

As you will have guessed, even if you have not solved the problem, Caroline was not guessing. She wrote a letter to the Personnel Department in these terms:

> Dear Sir,
>
> I am told that Mr Poker complained that I was guessing about the labels on the boxes of grotchets and mongles, but I was not.
>
> I opened the box marked 'grotchets and mongles' and looked at one item. It was a mongle. Since I was told that all three boxes were wrongly labelled, that had to be the mongle box. That left two boxes, one containing mongles and grotchets and one containing only grotchets. But one of the boxes was already labelled 'grotchets' and therefore could not contain grotchets by themselves. It had to contain grotchets and mongles, and the third box, wrongly labelled 'mongles' had to contain grotchets.
>
> I was therefore able to label all three boxes correctly without opening the other two.
>
> Yours sincerely,
>
> Caroline Penser.

When Caroline's mother saw the letter she said, 'Stupid child. Never make trouble.'

But Caroline got a letter from the Works Manager asking her to come and see him about the possibility of joining the design department as an apprentice in the drawing office. He also asked if she would be interested in attending day release classes in design and technology. There was no mention of the box labels.

A33. Poles apart together (Q3)

The illustration on the left shows how I managed to get six poles all touching. Georgie got seven poles all touching by setting one upright.

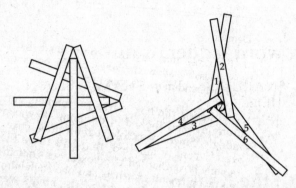

We were fools because we could have solved the puzzle in the comfort of the pub using pencils or cigarettes instead of heaving fenceposts about and annoying the neighbours. That is, providing we assume that drinking alcohol in pubs is better than good exercise for brain and muscles in the open air. Otherwise, ...

You are only young once, and not for long then.

A34. What is the rule? (Q14)

The answer is 'BEVEL'. The rule is that the words alternately begin and end with the successive letters of the alphabet. Any word ending in 'L' would do, and the next word in the list would begin with 'M'.

Harold was angry all the way home, awkwardly carrying two jam jars of wriggling fish, two nets and a tin of bait. But he had to admit it was a good rule. He got Cecil's arithmetic homework wrong, but whether on purpose or not I cannot tell.

A35. Make do and mend (Q85)

The NOTABLE doctor was NOT ABLE to operate because there was NO TABLE.

A36. A word ladder (Q76)

SNAIL – SNARL – SNARE – SHARE – SHAKE – SHALE – SHALL – SHELL.

A37. All the Ks (Q67)

Here they are; they are all in the dictionary – all 20. Give yourself 100 points if you have found some that Ken did not.

Kangaroo	Koa	Kill	Knurl
Kohl	Kurd	Kudos	Knight
Knob	Knit	Kopek	Kit
Kite	Kip	Knap	Ken
Knee	Kitten	Kine	Kin

A38. As ? is to ? so is ? to ? (Q58)

The answer is A.

Colour swaps and number swaps are the same, but there has been a vertical and horizontal flip which is consistent.

A39. Odd one out (Q49)

If you are looking this up you have probably not solved it, and are therefore dead. I do not speak to corpses. But for those who did solve it and are just checking up:-

5645 is the intruder. All the others are exactly divisible by nine. The only way to check that in the time is to total the five digits in each case and see if that total is exactly divisible by nine. If it is, the whole number is. The same is true of dividing by three.

A40. Another phrase-word (Q94)

'Olive! Let Young Men Pay In Cash.'

A41. Crossword for the clueless (Q41)

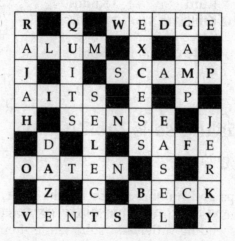

A42. The A-Z of X-words (Q32)

The lazy dog provided this solution. He cheated a bit. He did not know several of the words, but found them in the computer dictionary.

Many thousands of typists who key this familiar sentence now know that they are uttering a falsehood, it is no longer so. True to his wager, the Quick Brown Fox no longer jumps over the Lazy Dog.

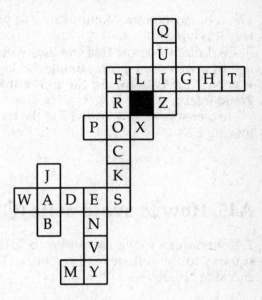

A43. Battle of the series (Q23)

The answer to Lady Pamela's problem was '30 and 42'. The formula is

$$n^2 - n$$

with the integers from 1 upwards (i.e., subtracting the rising integers from their squares).

The answer to Professor Kalkalus' problem was '294 and 1282'. The formula is

$$n^3 - n^2$$

where n is the rising prime numbers (i.e., taking the prime numbers in ascending order and subtracting their squares from their cubes).

A44. Three dice (Q4)

The top and bottom of any dice always totals seven, whichever way it is lying.

Cecil did not know that the dice with '1' showing was chosen and thrown a second time, but he did know that whichever dice it was both the bottom and the top of it had been included in the grand total.

He therefore simply added 7 to the total that he could see – 15 – making 22.

A45. How to avoid mate (Q15)

1. Roberto can move the white rook (on king's knight 6) four squares to the left, revealing check. The black rook takes the checking bishop.

2. The apparent oddity about the position is that both white bishops are on white squares.

3. A pawn may be promoted to a queen *or any other piece*. This position could be reached, therefore, if the bishop which started on a black square was captured, and a subsequent pawn promotion was used to create a second bishop on a white square.

A46. Use all you've got (Q86)

1674 / 93 x 5 + 2 - 80 = 12

A47. A bright idea (Q77)

The standard way was to cut the wedges one at a time length-wise. I wanted to cut several at once across the thickness.

I tilted the bandsaw table to the slight angle required, and took a pack of five of the cross cut stock pieces (3" along the grain x 6" x 1"). I then cut the pack through the 3" way, turning the pack top for bottom each pass. In this way I cut five wedges at a pass.

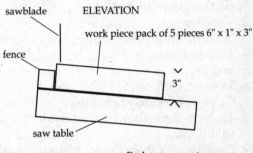

Pack moves past saw away from reader

A48. The majority below average? (Q68)

I was a wood-machinist in the twenties, before there was much concern for safety. When I went to the Union meeting and saw them hold up their hands to vote I could see that the average number of fingers for that group was perhaps eight or eight and a half each.

So the average number of fingers in the population must be below ten, because although there are a few people born with excess fingers, there are many more who have lost one or more fingers. The average number of fingers per person may therefore be 9.99 or even less, but the vast majority of people have ten.

Is there any instance the other way round? The average number of motor cars owned by members of the world population may be less than one-tenth of a car per person. Clearly, however, the vast majority own no car. Any answer on these lines is good.

A49. General unwanted knowledge (Q59)

1. Shakespeare's Othello.
2. Victoria.
3. Sodium chloride.
4. Gerald Ford.
5. 960.
6. Denver, Colorado.
7. Ceylon, formerly Serendip.
8. Hobart. Tasmania is an island to the south of the Australian mainland.
9. Greenwich Observatory Museum in Greenwich Park, which is a Royal Park and thus Crown Property.
10. They are medullary rays (extending radially from the pith) which are unusually thick in oak.

A50. Making your points (Q95)

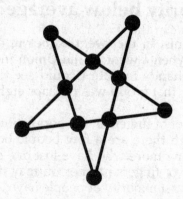

A51. How much wood in a log? (Q51)

Hoppus had it all round his girth! His formula puts the value of π as 4. Believe it or not, the whole timber trade around the world, led by the Brits, has worked on this assumption for centuries.

Here is the caculation for the first question, comparing a Hoppus foot with a cubic foot.

$$\frac{\text{Volume V(Hoppus)} = L(D/4)^2}{\text{True Volume v} \quad = \pi r^2 L}$$

Cancelling out we get $4/\pi = 1.27324$ cubic feet.

Thus every Hoppus cubic foot contains 1.27324 true cubic feet.

The log in question had 65.7222 Hoppus feet and therefore 51.618 true cubic feet.

Now for the hard question. The formula for the volume of a truncated cone is given below. You need to know the radius at either end, R and r, and the length, L.

$$\text{Volume } V = 1/3 \; \pi L(R^2 + r^2 + rR)$$

This means that taking the girth at the centre gives a further serious overmeasurement.

No one dares to tell anyone in the timber trade that they have the biggest cubic feet in the world. But prices reflect the actual value of the wood and comparative volumes. As long as a consistent measure of volume is applied, it all comes right in the market.

A52. Another scrambled aphorism (Q42)

High intelligence is no defence against stupidity.

A53. A problem with a virus (Q33)

This is the correct sum.

What the virus introduced by Hacker had done was to subtract 12 from the ASCII codes for the digits 0-9, producing the various symbols such as brackets and the dollar sign.

	4	1	8	0
	5	2	9	1
	6	3	0	2
	7	4	1	3
	8	5	2	4
	9	6	3	5
4	1	3	4	5

A54. Dividing land for heirs (Q24)

This is how it was done. The hedge along the north side of the plot at the south west corner of the garden was turned through an angle of 90°, and the hedge on the western edge of the plot at the north west corner of the garden was also turned through 90°.

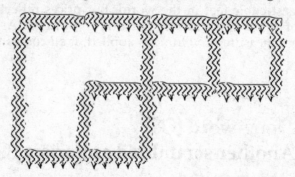

Fortunately, the hedges survived this treatment and continued to flourish for years to come.

A55. Puzzle for life (Q5)

You have only your body – and its products. One of these, you must guess which, is a fluid with which, in time, you can fill the hole and float the rubber ball and the attached key up to your eager but slightly squeamish fingers.

We are taught as children not to play with what we excrete. The idea of using it, instead of just getting rid of it, is strange to most people. The aliens killed those who were incapable of such lateral thinking.

A56. Shrimpoas (Q16)

The three aphorisms are:

1. NATURE USES AS LITTLE AS POSSIBLE OF ANYTHING. KEPLER
2. NATURE NEVER BREAKS HER OWN LAWS. DA VINCI
3. HE WHO CANNOT LOVE MUST LEARN TO FLATTER. GOETHE

A57. Multiply to reverse (Q87)

21978 x 4 = 87912

A58. A long word (Q78)

There may be much longer words – hundreds of marks if you find one – but this is pretty long:

ENCYCLOPAEDIAS

You should say 'Tut' if you left off the plural 's'.

A59. Classes in grammar (Q69)

The two groups are: slowly, rapidly, carefully and slightly, friendly, spindly. The former are adverbs, used to qualify a verb or 'do word'. The latter are adjectives used to describe or qualify nouns – 'person or thing words'.

A60. A frequent business lie (Q96)

'The cheque is in the post.' It briefly gets the creditor off the phone so that you can get on with raising the money to pay into the bank. It infuriates the creditor.

A61. Einstein quotation (Q61)

'Great spirits have always found violent opposition from mediocrities. The latter cannot understand it when a man does not thoughtlessly submit to hereditary prejudices but honestly and courageously uses his intelligence and fulfils the duty to express the results of his thoughts in clear form.'

A62. Can they be random? (Q52)

All six series could be part of a longer random series. As Karl Popper has pointed out, any of them might be part of a random series and will for certain be part of any infinite random series. If you go on writing random numbers long enough, any short series you choose will be repeated many times if, and only if, the series is truly random.

A63. Sort this lot out (Q43)

These are the two classes:
1. imitate, try, speculate 2. aphorism, monkey, idea
The first are 'do-words' or verbs as old fogies say. The second are 'name-words' or nouns, which designate a thing or abstraction to which verbs can be applied.

A64. Every which way (Q34)

The following cities appear in the grid: BONN, NICE, MADRID, MALAGA, ANKARA, LISBON, HULL, BOMBAY, SEATTLE, CARDIFF, KIEV, NAPLES, TEL AVIV, LIMA, CAIRO, GDANSK, PERTH, MILAN, ROME, TOKYO.

A65. Throw out the gatecrasher (Q25)

The gatecrasher is Ernest Rutherford. He was a physicist; the others were chemists.

A66. Getting serious about series (Q6)

Professor Kalkalus' answer was '120'. His fifth member of the series was zero, which was of course both trivial and a joke. Lady Pamela did not see it, and sulked grimly for hours.

This absurd nonsense has absorbed and confused mathematicians since Euler. Someone took ages to show that there might be a further integer in the series, with thousands of digits. Later, someone else spent ages and lots of computer time to prove conclusively that there are no further members of the series.

Product one less than a square! Pshaw!

A67. Help a deprived poem (Q17)

The Air that God did freely give
We all must breathe that we may live.
Aerobic unobstructed breath
Ensureth Health, delayeth death.
But air that's forced through vocal chords,
Deformed and tortured into words
By being muddled up among
Thy cheeks and throat and teeth and tongue,
Imposes such a gruesome strain
On epiglottis, tongue and brain
That I advise, nay more, insist,
That thou forbear, belt up! desist.
Be silent. Speak not. Hold thy tongue
From birth till final dirge be sung.

But wait, I had forgotten. Yes!
There's one exception, I confess.
Unless thy sad and sorry fate
Shall be to meet and know and hate
A monster of that horrid breed
Whose plans and ventures all succeed.
For verbal noise may be excused,
And speech itself may well be used
To castigate and put those down
Who are admired around the Town.
So, Speakers must be ever blamed,
Save where achievers may be shamed.
The Rule of Dumbness may be broke
To hurt and humble able folk.

A68. Misunderstanding foreigners (Q88)

Let Us Forget That Hatred And Nastiness Surround All.

A69. Scepticism (Q79)

John Dalton – Chemist – a founder of chemical theory
Theodor Schwann – physiologist – first elaborated cell theory in
    biology
Gregor Mendel – priest and biologist – first established the laws
    of genetics
Ernest Rutherford – physicist – the first to split the atom
Francis Crick – biochemist – discovered the coiled chemical
    structure of the genome
Claud Shannon – mathematician – founded modern information
    theory
Dmitri Mendeleyev – chemist – discovered the periodic tables

A70. Square the difference (Q97)

The Professor had challenged Lady Pamela to prove her claim.

'It is so very simple, my love,' she said, drawling slowly. 'Take any two consecutive integers. Got that, my sweet?'

'Go on. I'm not a primary pupil.'

'Multiply the smaller by -1, and there you are!'

He watched as she scribbled with her red lipstick on the black silk bedsheet.

$$(a^2 - a) = (b^2 - b)$$
Take 6 and 7
$$6 \times -1 = -6$$
$$-6^2 = +36$$
The difference between -6 and 36 is 42
$$7^2 - 7 = 49 - 7 = 42$$

The Professor got wearily from the four-poster bed.

'True of any two consecutive integers, my dear love,' said Lady Pamela. 'Bring the ash-tray as you come, my dear man; and why not the soothing little Moet with the glasses. I am sure you need it.'

He lit her Corona and served the champagne, morosely plotting puzzles.

A71. Difficult definitions (Q71)

Neoplasm = 17 (Unexpected new tissue as in cancer)
Infatuated = 16 (Inspired with extravagant passion)
Infinite = 5 (Limitless)
Retrogressive = 12 (Reactive, retreating from advance)
Hegemony = 14 (Leadership of a confederacy)
Inchoate = 15 (Unformed, just begun)
Turbid = 4 (Unclear)
Turgid = 11 (Morbidly swollen)
Livid = 13 (Leaden bluish coloured)
Genome = 18 (The entire set of chromosomes in a cell)

A72. The characters of the chess pieces (Q62)

Ermyntrude failed to solve this, but she was only seven at the time. The solution is shown opposite.

Ermyntrude shook her head when she was shown this. She said that the Bishops and Queens were too powerful. Both Queens should be deposed, and the Kings should form an alliance and call an election.

A73. Teddy's funny tots (Q53)

Teddy's answer was: $1 = 2$, $4 = 4$, $9 = 6$.

The 'context' Teddy referred to is the usual LED display of numbers such as on a digital clock or a calculator. One is shown by 2 bars, four has 4 bars and nine has 6 bars, as the full list of digits below illustrates.

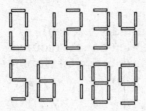

A74. Seeking connections (Q44)

The connecting thought is 'OLD'.

The four clues point to:

An OLD salt

OLD Glory, the American flag

The OLD Man of the Sea, who clung to the back of
Sinbad the Sailor

OLD Lang Syne, sung in a ring to greet each New Year

A75. Catching Caroline (Q35)

It was an old trick question for draughtsmen, but Caroline had not only found the usual answer but a second one they did not know, but which was equally valid. Hacker sheepishly explained that it was a drawing office trick which every novice had to face.

'That's quite OK, Sir. A sort of initiation challenge. I quite understood.' He did not like the 'understood' but let it pass.

Next day Hacker told the juniors that Caroline was a clever girl and had almost got it right. Then he challenged them to find an alternative solution to the problem. When they failed, he casually showed them his new solution. 'Old Hacker certainly knows his stuff,' they said.

This is what Caroline drew, with the more well-known solution on the left.

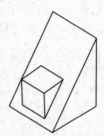 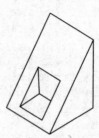

A76. Powerful schoolboys (Q26)

'The only way I can explain it,' said Teddy, 'is that the speed of light squared is an acceleration – metres per second (m/s) becomes m^2/s^2, whatever that means. Multiply by a mass and you have a force. Express this over a distance and you acquire energy.'

Teddy did the sum like this.

$$E = Mc^2$$
Let's take mass to be 1 kg
$$E = 1 \text{ kg} \times c^2$$
$$c = 3 \times 10^8 \text{ m/s}$$
$$E = 1 \text{ kg} \times (3 \times 10^8 \text{ m/s})^2$$
or $9 \times 10^{16} \text{ kg m}^2/\text{s}^2$

This expression – kg m^2/s^2 – troubled Tommy. 'What is a kilogram metre squared per second squared?' he demanded.

'I've looked it up,' said Teddy. A Newton – the measure of force – is kilogram metre per second per second (kg m/s^2). A joule – the measure of power – is Newtons multiplied by metres or power times distance (J = Nm). So a joule is a kg m^2/s^2 and there are 9 x 10^{16} of them in a kilogram of mass, according to our equation.

'There you are,' said Tommy. 'I weigh 50 kg and have 50 times that much power, and you have a mere 45 times as much.' He did some work on the calculator. 'There you are! I am the more powerful. I have 4.5 x 10^5 terajoules of power, while you have a mere 4.05 x 10^5.'

'I'd like to know the answer in megawatt hours,' said Teddy.

'A watt is a joule per second, so divide by 3600 seconds in the hour, and then divide by a million to get megawatts, and there you are. A bit over ten billion megawatt hours, I'd say. We are powerful, very much so!'

The new headmaster found them poring over their papers. He regarded them with a mixture of severity and puzzled concern. Under his gaze, they suddenly felt less powerful. The head did not understand applied mathematics, and told them to get on with their reading.

Later on he looked up 'terajoules'. 'A million million joules,' he muttered. 'I'll have to do something about those lads.'

A77. Classifying clouds (Q7)

There are two independent ways of ordering the clouds, and you have to give both ways to be correct.

They are: by the number of bulges and by size. The diagram overleaf shows the correct order under both classifications.

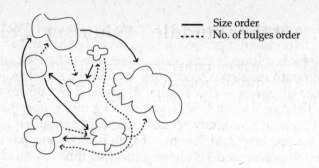

A78. Building a magic cube (Q18)

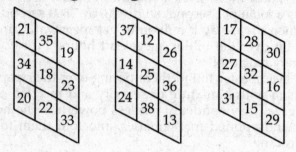

A79. More connections (Q89)

B. Each separate feature changes consistently with the example.

A80. Another scrambled quotation (Q98)

'Under this stone, Reader, survey
Dead Sir John Vanbrugh's house of clay.
Lie heavy on him, earth, for he
Laid many a heavy load on thee.'

A81. Another muddled aphorism (Q81)

'The world must be rather a rough place for clever people. Ordinary folk dislike them, and as for themselves, they hate each other most cordially.' *J. K. Jerome*

A82. Connections (Q72)

The keyword is 'WHITE'. The clues referred to the white ball in snooker, whitewashing, Snow White and the White House.

A83. Relationships (Q63)

A. The two figures are reversed in order and turned top to bottom.

A84. A disagreeable word (Q54)

With this sort of question and ingenuity you can make any one the odd one out. But the simplest answer is TEACH.

The remaining words in the list can be used as nouns *or* verbs. For example, you *cash* a cheque, and thus can have *cash* in your pocket; you can *hammer* a nail into a piece of wood using an instrument called a *hammer*. But whilst you can *teach* somebody, you cannot have a *teach*.

A85. Listing deprived lists (Q45)

The precocious young rascal had been listing various 'list' words from the Thesaurus, but perversely leaving out alternate letters and marking the gaps with a period. The complete list was:

1. Catalogue
2. Inventory
3. Thesaurus
4. Programme
5. Almanac
6. Dictionary
7. Glossary
8. Lexicon
9. Gazetteer
10. Roster
11. Schedule
12. Register

A86. Metamorphosis (Q36)

These are the words created by expanding the animals at either end:

1. PARAPETED
2. OPERATION
3. FURCATION
4. INFANTILE
5. PRECURSOR
6. HYPHENATE
7. FAREWELLS

A87. Lady Pamela's revenge (Q27)

8	1.5	1	6.5
2.5	5	5.5	4
4.5	3	3.5	6
2	7.5	7	0.5

A week after being given the problem, Professor Kalkalus accused Lady Pamela of setting an impossible problem. She sent him her answer, and after a furious argument he followed the hounds with her a week later.

This is the crafty solution that trapped him into going with Lady Pamela to the hunt.

The Professor argued that fractions were illegitimate, until she reminded him of his underhand use of negative integers in a previous magic square problem.

He was a competent rider and enjoyed the hunt. They found just once, but the fox went to ground and there was no kill. The Professor looked flushed and pleased with himself at the animal's escape. But Lady Pamela was pleased enough. She had seen the hunter-tribesman within trying to get out, yes, even from the right, tight, know-it-all professor.

A88. Little to help you (Q8)

Face up to it – it is a question of how many faces each object has. A sphere has one continuous face, a cone has two, a solid cylinder has three, a hollow cylinder has four, a tetrahedron has five, etc.

If you arranged the objects in the line as shown below, you live.

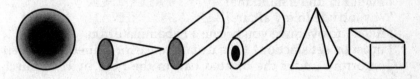

A89. Nesting spheres (Q19)

I know you will say I am cheating, but I am not.

No more than three marbles can be arranged so that all touch all. True; but my father made a different generalisation. 'Only three spheres will 'nest', each touching the other two,' he said. He spoke of spheres, not spheres of equal radius like marbles.

You can nest four spheres if they are of different radii. For instance, in the space between a castle of three billiard balls you could nest another small sphere. You have to be careful!

A90. Same across, same down (Q99)

S	L	A	P
L	A	N	E
A	N	T	E
P	E	E	R

A91. The duel (Q91)

'I understand you undertake to overthrow all my undertakings.'
   'Fie! I intend to overtake you in everything.'
   'You are insulting!'
   'I intend it, understand me?'
   'Why intrude in my affairs?'
   'I intend to overawe you because I abominate you.'
   'I insist on satisfaction.' (The usual phrase for a duel challenge.)
   'Tomorrow under the blasted oak in the field by the church before dawn.' (The appointment for the duel.)

A92. More connections (Q82)

The connection is the word 'fiddle', the colloquial term for a swindle.

The other clues refer to 'Fiddler on the Roof', 'Fiddle-sticks!' and Nero, who fiddled while Rome burned.

A93. A well forgotten phrase (Q73)

'Russia, self outcast, sharpens her bayonets in her arctic night and mechanically proclaims through self starved lips her philosophy of hatred and death.'

This was said by Winston Churchill when he was in the political wilderness in the thirties.

A94. How to put things right (Q64)

Fireman. Hesitant. Together.

A95. On the hunt for birds (Q55)

Here they are, all twenty-one birds. I hope you did not get them by comparing notes with other Wild Watchers. That is what half of them have done.

Blackbird,	Rook,	Crow,	Sparrow,
Starling,	Thrush,	Gannet,	Seagull,
Owl,	Pigeon,	Swallow,	Kingfisher,
Kite,	Plover,	Pheasant,	Dove,
Tit,	Gull,	Jay,	Auk,
Dodo			

What? All in one place? In a rain forest? At the same season? They were stuffed! How obliging of the enterprising firm, Wildwatch Unlimited, Inc.

A96. The one that is left behind (Q46)

With teasing hesitations, fake corrected mistakes, and long
pauses, whilst all the while chattering vivaciously, Lady Pamela
took away the seven matches that revealed the following pattern:

The Professor was white with fury. He looked as though he
might be violent, then went red, raged and swore. 'Insufferable,
snooty, unprincipled, cheating woman,' he almost screamed. He
went on in this vein for some time; I dare not reveal the language.

Heads turned at other tables. A few people stood up, staring.
The head waiter began to hover. The Professor gritted his teeth
and went silent. Lady Pamela was enthralled. Deeply moved and
excited, she sat gazing into his angry, hating eyes with clear
delight.

It is not revealed whether that was the night of the Surrender of
Her All. That is another and private puzzle, the answer to which
you are not invited to attempt. But I know what I know!

A97. Keeping Ermyntrude occupied (Q37)

This is the solution to the word square
that Ermyntrude failed to solve. Did
you fail?

E	R	A	S	E	S
R	E	M	O	V	E
A	M	E	L	I	A
S	O	L	E	N	T
E	V	I	N	C	E
S	E	A	T	E	R

A98. Squaring the pyramid (Q28)

Teddy had not lost his marbles; he had won 20 from Tommy. This is how he did it.

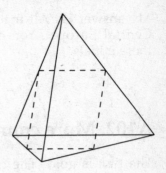

Take a linear vertex and draw a line parallel and central on the two faces that make that vertex. If you cut through both lines you will have divided the tetrahedron equally, leaving two square faces.

A99. Bring back the magic (Q9)

17	4	3	14
6	11	12	9
10	7	8	13
5	16	15	2

This is the corrected magic square. Each row, column and diagonal adds up to 38.

To destroy the magic, I rotated the outer square of 12 numbers one place anti-clockwise, and the inner square of 4 numbers two places clockwise.

Don't let me know if you succeeded. It will only upset me.

A100. Spotting faulty boxes (Q100)

Three of the boxes could not have been made up from Caroline's drawing. They are A, B and D.

A101. Another airline phraseword (Q111)

My answer is: 'All Ingest Ravishing Food Right Around North Central Europe'. You might have found a better phrase using these initials.

A102. More connections (Q120)

The link is gold. The clues refer to gold itself used as money, referred to by the Apostle Paul as 'filthy lucre'; the Golden Calf which Aaron made; the Golden Horn at the entrance to the Bosphorus; and the Golden Fleece.

A103. Coping with the unknown again (Q130)

The missing total is 30, and the values are:

$$W = 7.25 \quad X = 4.25 \quad Y = 9.25 \quad Z = 8.25$$

A104. Dolly and dirty (Q140)

Every reconstituted cigarette leaves its own cigarette end. 3456 butts at six per roll equals 576 cigarettes, but 576 butts make a further 96 cigarettes, and the 96 butts from these make a further 16 cigarettes, and these in turn yield another two. This is a total of 690 cigarettes, two more than the 688 required at 98 per day for seven days.

Dolly was right when she was sober. Were you?

A105. Some four-letter words (Q150)

The correct definitions are as follows:

1.	aeon	an age of the universe
2.	Ainu	a hairy tribe
3.	ankh	Egyptian symbol, key-like cross
4.	brae	steep bank
5.	craw	crop of bird or insect
6.	dahl	dish from dried peas (Indian)
7.	yean	to give birth to (lamb or goat)
8.	dory	flat bottomed skiff (boat)
9.	nous	intelligence, 'savvy'
10.	loon	scamp, boor (arch.)
11.	spay	castrate
12.	souk	North African market

A106. Ask a silly question . . . (Q160)

This is what Harold wrote:

Ball weighs 100lbs/half its weight. Let w = true weight.
Then w = 100lbs/0.5w
Multiply both sides by w
w x w = w x 100lbs/0.5w
Now simplify by cancelling out w on the right hand side
w^2 = 100lbs/0.5 = 200lbs
w = $\sqrt{200}$lbs = 14.14213lbs

'Have we got it right, Sir,' asked Harold, 'or is it just another silly mistake?' They had, of course, got it right and after this incident Dr Surd began to treat the two bright lads with more respect.

A107. Can you count? (Q170)

It is confusing, but there are ten circles and ten rectangles including the frame. I have to admit that I could not have counted them myself, if I hadn't kept a record as I drew them in on my PC.

A108. Riddle-me-ree (Q154)

Too simple! It was a splinter in his foot.

A109. Shrimpoas 3 (Q145)

1. Who does not enjoy solitude will not love freedom. *Schopenhauer*
2. Better be quarrelling than lonesome. *Irish Proverb*
3. Each social class has its own pathology. *Proust*

A110. Head transplants (Q110)

The word is 'holiday', and you deserve one if you got it.

HAND	HANG
OATH	OAST
LAKE	LACE
ITEM	ION
DAMP	DALE
AIDE	AKIN
YANK	YAWN

A111. Square up to this (Q101)

B	A	T	O	N
A	R	O	M	A
T	O	N	E	S
O	M	E	G	A
N	A	S	A	L

A field marshal's or conductor's baton

The last letter of the Greek alphabet

A112. Connections (Q112)

The connecting theme is 'seven', which is an odd prime number. The clues refer to: the Seven Dwarves, the Seven Wonders of the World, the Seven Deadly Sins, and the winning throw at the dice game 'Shooting Craps'.

A113. Connections yet again (Q136)

The connection is feather. The clues refer to the white feather handed to young men who did not join up in the First World War; feathering one's nest; feathering the oars in rowing; and the three feathers of the coat of arms of the Prince of Wales, who has been a critic of modern architects.

A114. My joust with Johnny Carson (Q174)

I gave the answer 'three' for socks, because if the first two were different colours the third must make a pair of either colour.

But when he said 'three' for gloves I said, 'Three right-hand ones?' That was the end of the show but Johnny was a great performer and his clever reaction got all the applause and sympathy. I was cast as the cocky clever-clogs, but American Mensa got sixty-five thousand applications.

With gloves you could, with bad luck, get twelve black left-hand and twelve white right-hand, so you must take 25 to be sure of a pair.

A115. Even more connections (Q165)

The connection is 'king'. The clues refer to the King's Evil (scrofula – so-called because it was thought the king could cure it); the tiger – the 'king of the jungle'; Old King Cole with his pipe, bowl and three fiddlers; and King Kong.

A116. Further connections (Q156)

The linking idea is 'fall'. The references are to the Niagara Falls; 'fall' which is the North American term for autumn; the fall that follows pride; and fall-out following an atomic chain reaction.

A117. How much science do you know? (Q147)

Here are the correct definitions:

a.	an ohm	the measure of electrical resistance
b.	epistemology	the science of knowledge
c.	a sigmoid curve	an 'S'-shaped curve in mathematics
d.	palaeontology	the science and study of fossils
e.	entomology	the science and study of insects
f.	a genome	the full set of genes in a cell
g.	a phylum	a major biological taxonomy division
h.	a fulcrum	the support upon which a lever operates
i.	a cantilever	an end-supported horizontal structure
j.	a normal curve	a gaussian, or bell, curve
k.	cosmology	the science of the universe
l.	a farad	the S.I. unit of electrical capacitance

A118. Sorting and ranking (Q138)

This is how the items should be arranged:

Microcosm.
>   8 quark   10 electron   1 atom   2 molecule   5 crystal

These are the physical entities in order of size and mass.

Macrocosm.
>   3 meteorite   11 meteor   6 planet   4 star   7 galaxy   9 universe

These are the astronomic bodies in order of size and mass.

A119. The statistical approach (Q129)

Given the absurd assumption that all 20 sheep are shorn on one side and are facing both ways yet all showing the shorn side, the probability is rather low. For each sheep the probability $p = 0.5$, for 20 sheep it is 0.5^{20} = about one in ten million ($p = 9.53674 \times 10^{-7}$ to be exact).

But again on the unlikely assumption that there is one half shorn sheep there, it is an evens chance that the unshorn side will be turned away. So beware of overcautious assumptions. Sheep farming is not like that, and we all know it.

A120. Cryptic clued ten-word square (Q172)

	1	2	3	4	5
1	S	P	O	T	S
2	M	O	R	A	L
3	A	L	A	T	E
4	R	A	T	E	D
5	T	R	E	S	S

A121. Placing digits (Q121)

The correct answer is: $468 \times 1 + 32 = 500$

Mrs Char was delighted when she was able to show her answer to Ermyntrude. 'There you are, my child. Try not to get your bricks mixed up in future.'

'Oooh!' said Ermyntrude, 'You are clever, Mrs Char.'

A122. Phraseword for Eastern Airlines (Q102)

There may be better phrases than mine, which is:

'Everyone Allows Some Travel East Right Now'

A123. So square this one away, then (Q113)

P	A	R	I	S
A	V	A	S	T
R	A	S	S	E
I	S	S	U	E
S	T	E	E	D

A nautical term meaning 'Hold hard!'

A kind of civet cat.

A124. Black and white (Q108)

The large cube cannot be formed from a number of the smaller double cubes. There are twenty-seven small cubes in the larger cube, and thus 13 double cubes will be needed, plus one odd black cube.

A125. Numerical relations (Q175)

B. Each number is reversed and 1 is added to each digit.

A126. A ten-word square (Q166)

	6	7	8	9	10
1	S	L	I	N	K
2	W	O	M	A	N
3	O	V	A	T	E
4	R	E	G	A	L
5	D	R	O	L	L

A127. Wonky weighing (Q157)

My answer was 9.33 x (2.93/3.62) = 7.552 tonnes.

A128. Logical triangles (Q148)

The missing figure is 50. In each triangle the top figure times the bottom-left figure minus the bottom-right figure equals the centre.

A129. Spotting the right spots (Q139)

James was pleased because Kwizzer had fallen into his trap. There are three, not two, other logically correct locations for spots and Kwizzer had missed the third. Did you?

He faxed Kwizzer the correct solution, as opposite, with a black ring around the spot that had been omitted. He marked it 'stupidly obvious?', with no other comment.

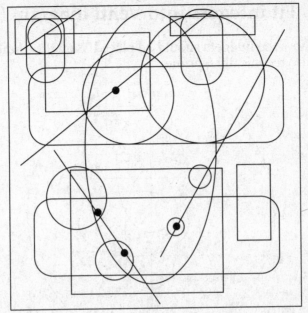

The correct spots are all within a rectangle, a round-cornered rectangle, a circle and an ellipse and on a line.

A130. Related domino triplets (Q173)

The answer is D. Each set of dominoes comprises 6 cells. Comparing each individual cell, the changes from those in C to those in D are the same as the changes between the corresponding cells in A and B.

For example, the first domino in A is a 3:2 and the first in B is a 5:4; so two has been added to each cell. Similarly, if you add 2 to each cell of the first domino in C (1:2) you get 3:4, the first domino in D.

A131. Fit integers into Venn diagram (Q131)

This is how the integers should be placed. Nought counts as even and is also technically a prime.

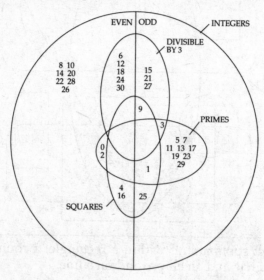

A132. Snap chances (Q122)

With such problems it is simpler to calculate the chances against the event.

The probability of a blank round with no 'snap' is:-

$$51/52^{52} = 0.9807692 \text{ to the power of } 52$$

This yields the answer p = 0.364314

So the chance of a snap is 63.569% per round of 52 pairs

A133. Altered synonyms and antonyms (Q103)

1.	Hate	Scorn	Detest	Adore	Worship	Love
2.	Grand	Vast	Great	Puny	Scanty	Small
3.	Dull	Faint	Drab	Light	Glaring	Bright
4.	Good	Just	Kind	Bad	Poor	Grave

A134. Shattered crossword (Q114)

A135. More imaginary folding & cutting (Q163)

This is what Caroline drew. It was not 'near enough' – it was correct.

A136. I tangle with the Barracuda (Q176)

The correct answer is 'Either or both A and D'.

Any other answer is incomplete. You have to make the sights point at where the bullets are hitting. These are all the actions which will do so.

A137. Numberless assignation (Q167)

The Professor turned up – a bit late – at number 76. It was a splendid old mansion with an enormous open log fire, on which the food was cooked. The steak and the subsequent proceedings, which involved the large bearskin rug in front of the fire, were well worth the hassle.

A138. Mental paperwork (Q158)

This is what you should have drawn or described if you have a very good imagination.

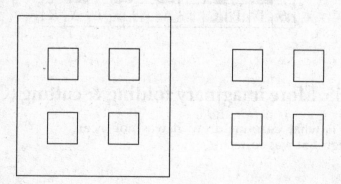

A139. Crossword jigsaw (Q149)

C	U	R	A	R	E	█	P	A	L	L	I	D
U	█	E	█	E	X	P	E	L	█	A	█	R
R	E	P	E	N	T	█	N	O	O	D	L	E
L	█	E	█	T	R	A	C	E	█	L	█	A
E	R	A	S	█	A	C	E	█	D	E	A	R
W	A	L	L	S	█	T	█	T	E	S	T	Y
█	V	█	O	I	L	█	P	I	N	█	T	.
S	E	T	O	N	█	T	█	P	E	D	A	L
C	L	I	P	█	T	I	M	█	S	E	R	E
A	█	M	█	S	H	E	E	T	█	P	█	S
R	E	B	A	T	E	█	R	I	D	E	R	S
E	█	E	█	U	R	G	E	D	█	N	█	E
D	E	R	I	D	E	█	S	E	E	D	E	R

A140. Continued sustainable growth (Q109)

The sequence is:

A AT EAT HEAT HEATH SHEATH SHEATHE SHEATHED

My guess is that in this case growth is not sustainable, but you may prove me wrong.

A141. The Professor's revenge (Q141)

This is the result when real instead of imaginary paper and scissors are used.

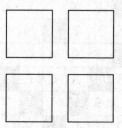

A142. The tragedy of scholarship (Q132)

Literally, I am a bookworm.

A143. Spot spotting (Q123)

All three spots are inside big and small triangles, two rectangles and a circle. There is no other place where a spot can fulfil these conditions.

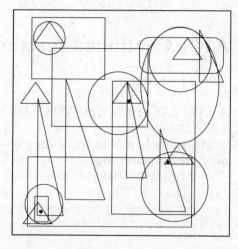

A144. Throw the odd ones out (Q104)

The intruders are 110, which should be moved from A to C; 35, which should be moved from B to A; and 120, which should be moved from C to B.

The correct series are thus:

A. 0, 6, 35, 143, 323, 667
B. 24, 72, 120, 210, 288, 420
C. 0, 6, 20, 42, 72, 110, 156

Series A is the product of successive pairs of prime numbers: 0 and 1, 2 and 3, 5 and 7, 11 and 13, etc.

Series B is the product of successive pairs of non-prime numbers: 4 and 6, 8 and 9, 10 and 12, 14 and 15, etc.

Series C is the product of successive pairs of integers: 0 and 1, 2 and 3, 4 and 5, 6 and 7, etc.

A145. You have no imagination (Q115)

The answer that 'Corny' failed to get is four right-angled triangles thus:

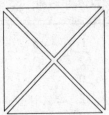

Lady Pamela taunted him as they trotted home. He said, 'There is a time and place for everything and on horseback on the downs is no place for scissors and paper riddles.'

'You want me always to do the expected?' she queried.

'Yes, always.'

Getting the last word in as usual, she said 'Wrong again, my love. If I were predictable you'd be bored to death in a week.'

A146. All at sixes and sevens (Q146)

V	A	R	I	E	T	Y
E	A	R	A	C	H	E
R	A	D	I	C	A	L
B	A	S	H	F	U	L
A	V	O	C	A	D	O
L	O	C	K	J	A	W

A147. Absurdly meticulous pouring (Q177)

The minimum number of pourings is eight, as follows:

Jug capacity	2	5	7	12
Start	0	5	7	0
Step 1	2	3	7	0
Step 2	0	3	7	2
Step 3	2	1	7	2
Step 4	0	1	7	4
Step 5	1	0	7	4
Step 6	1	5	2	4
Step 7	2	4	2	4
Step 8	0	4	4	4

A148. Many 'ands make light work (Q168)

A child had written 'I LUVE MUMMYANDDADDY'.

Her older sister said 'Soppy thing. You have not left any spaces between 'Mummy' and 'and' and 'and' and Daddy.'

This is five consecutive 'ands'. There must be many other similar answers.

A149. The aliens in doubt (Q159)

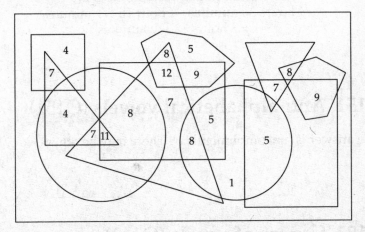

The rule is simple: count the sides of the figures. Each number is the total number of sides to the figures within which it is located. For example a dot inside a square is replaced with a 4, whereas a dot within a triangle and a square is replaced by a 7.

The aliens had failed to recognise a circle as a one-sided figure. This gave heart to the remaining human slaves of the aliens.

A150. How long to find out how long? (Q137)

To work out how long it should have taken:

Total the reciprocal of the normal time (in hours) for each worker

$$1/3 = 0.333$$
$$1/4 = 0.250$$
$$1/5 = \underline{0.200}$$
$$0.783$$

Now take the reciprocal of this figure
$$1/0.783 = 1.277 \text{ hours} = 1 \text{ hour } 16\,^1/2 \text{ minutes}$$

Therefore the wasted time was
4 hours 30 minutes - 1 hour 16 $^1/2$ minutes
= 3 hours 13 $^1/2$ minutes

A151. Anti-alphabetical vowels (Q151)

One answer is 'uncomplimentary'. There may be others.

A152. Square of words (Q142)

S	M	A	R	T
M	O	L	A	R
A	L	A	T	E
R	A	T	E	S
T	R	E	S	S

meaning 'winged'

A153. Early imagination (Q133)

This is what Lady Pamela described. She had not exactly cheated, but she had been prepared. She had been at it with paper and scissors herself.

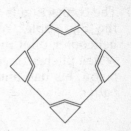

A154. Crossword jigsaw (Q124)

P	L	A	N	E	T		F	A	T	H	E	R
U		R		R	O	T	O	R		O		A
F	R	I	D	A	Y		R	U	N	L	E	T
F		S		S	E	R	U	M		D		H
I	C	E	D		D	I	M		M	E	R	E
N	O	S	E	D		M		B	O	R	E	R
	B		C	O	S		M	A	R		B	
C	R	O	O	N		L		G	A	S	E	S
H	A	I	R		C	O	G		Y	E	L	P
A		L		Z	E	B	R	A		V		E
S	P	I	C	E	D		A	P	P	E	A	L
E		N		R	A	I	N	S		R		L
S	I	G	N	O	R		D	E	T	E	R	S

245

A155. What? More connections? (Q105)

The connection is 'York'. The clues point to New York, known as the 'Big Apple'; York Minster; the Duke of York, who fought as a helicopter pilot in the Falklands War; a yorker, a ball in cricket which pitches directly by the batsman's feet and thus often passes below his bat; and Yorkshire Pudding, small portions of baked batter.

A156. The riddle of the Sphinx (Q116)

The answer is man, who first crawls on all fours, then walks on two legs, but in the evening of life needs a walking stick.

A157. Air combat tennis (Q155)

This is a kick-self calculation that looks difficult but is actually simple.

We know the missile's speed, so we are only concerned with the time that the missile is flying. That must be the time that the two planes take to meet. Their combined approach speed is 1600 mph. Therefore the time to their collision is:

$$500/1600 = 0.3125 \text{ hours.}$$

In this time the missile will travel

$$2000 \times 0.3125 \text{ miles} = 625 \text{ miles.}$$

A158. More spot spotting! (Q178)

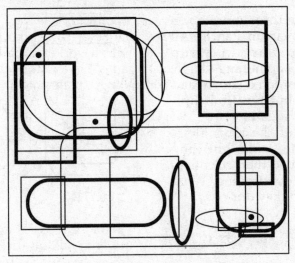

A159. Another head transplant job (Q169)

The word is 'SPRING'.

SING	SIFT
PACK	PACT
RED	REEL
IF	ICE
NAIL	NOTE
GOOD	GRIP

A160. An addled quotation (Q119)

'I cried all the way to the bank.' It was said by Liberace, the witty and resplendently dressed pianist.

A161. In similar circumstances (Q161)

There are three more spots in similar circumstances. All four spots are in a cup shape, a boomerang shape, a thick-bordered square and a circle, but not in a thin-bordered square.

None of the journalists found the spots, but they still pursued their relentless negative questioning. What else could they do?

A162. Not on the square (Q152)

T	R	A	M	P
R	A	D	A	R
A	D	O	R	E
M	A	R	R	Y
P	R	E	Y	S

A163. Antique puzzles revived (Q143)

'One misses his kisses and the other kisses his Missus.'

A164. Relationships (Q134)

A. Apathy (4)
B. File (3) – fork secures food while knife cuts, vice secures material for file to work on.

A165. Shrimpoas (Q125)

1. Arguments are to be avoided, they are always vulgar and often convincing. *Wilde*
2. Fashion wears out more apparel than the man. *Shakespeare*
3. There are occasions upon which all apology is rudeness. *Johnson*

A166. Department of trivial knowledge (Q106)

1. Almonds.
2. Icarus.
3. Bread, thin flat 'loaves'.
4. Ulan Bator, which means in Mongolian 'Red Hero'.
5. Constantinople, and before that Byzantium.
6. Adolf Hitler.
7. Atmospheric pressure.
8. Coventry, England.
9. The theory of Pythagoras, that states 'the hypotenuse squared equals the sum of the squares of the other two sides of a right-angled triangle'. If students could understand the proof, they passed over the 'bridge of asses'.
10. On the Egyptian coast west of Cairo. It was the turning point in World War II, when Montgomery defeated Rommel from there.

A167. Rank these prefixes (Q117)

The correct order from small to large is:-

atto, femto, pico, nano, micro, milli, centi, deci, deca, hecto, kilo, mega, giga, tera.

Here is the table from the BSI booklet *The Use of SI Units*.

Multiples and sub-multiples of units			

The names of the multiples and sub-multiples of the units are formed by means of the following prefixes:

Factor by which the unit is multiplied		Prefix	Symbol
1 000 000 000 000	= 10^{12}	tera	T
1 000 000 000	= 10^{9}	giga	G
1 000 000	= 10^{6}	mega	M
1 000	= 10^{3}	kilo	k
100	= 10^{2}	hecto	h
10	= 10^{1}	deca	da
0.1	= 10^{-1}	deci	d
0.01	= 10^{-2}	centi	c
0.001	= 10^{-3}	milli	m
0.000 001	= 10^{-6}	micro	μ
0.000 000 001	= 10^{-9}	nano	n
0.000 000 000 001	= 10^{-12}	pico	p
0.000 000 000 000 001	= 10^{-15}	femto	f
0.000 000 000 000 000 001	= 10^{-18}	atto	a

A168. The aliens falter (Q164)

The answer is fifty. Did you fail like the aliens? Or did you get all the possible sizes? And all the diagonal squares - both ways?

A169. Which is the odd one out? (Q179)

The last 4 is out of place, it should be 6. The numbers are what you have to add to each successive prime number to reach the next one.

These are the first few primes:

0, 1, 2, 3, 5, 7, 11, 13, 17, 19, 23, 29, 31, 37

(Note: Primes are not divisible exactly by any other integers apart from themselves and 1)

A170. Another resuscitated riddle (Q128)

'One roars with pain and the other pours with rain.'

If you already knew it, two points for remembering; if not, ten points for a good effort. Maybe you found a better answer.

A171. Still connections (Q171)

The connection is 'kiss'. The clues refer to kissing the rod; a kiss under the mistletoe; kissing the book (the Bible); and 'kiss and tell'.

A172. Simple addition? (Q162)

Our arabic numeral system works on powers of ten – the number of our fingers. We count the number of units, tens (10^1), hundreds (10^2), thousands (10^3) and so on.

The aliens worked in powers of five – a five-base system: units, 5^1, 5^2, 5^3, and so on. They arranged the rising powers of five concentrically outwards using the number of sides of a shape (up to four) to express the numerals. The figure 5 (arabic) was thus expressed as a circle inside an ellipse: i.e. 1 five and 0 units.

They used a circle, as we do, for nought (even though it has one side) and an ellipse for 1. A solid horizontal ellipse meant plus (+) and a vertical one meant equals (=).

The aliens' sum could therefore be expressed in arabic numerals thus:

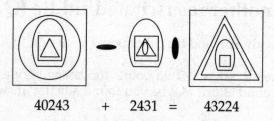

40243   +   2431 =   43224

Remember, when adding in base 5 if the total of two figures comes to more than 5 you deduct five, write the remainder, and carry one.

Written in denary, our base ten system, the sum would be:

$$\begin{array}{r} 2573 \\ 366 \\ \hline 2939 \end{array}$$

Did you survive?

A173. English through darts (Q153)

ANYWAY	BORZOI	GREYLY	QUORUM
ASLANT	CYCLIC	LASSOS	PESETA
BASALT	DOGGER	LESSEE	TABOUR
BEACON	FLAXEN	LYRICS	SUNDAE

A174. Finding a suitable position (Q144)

The two positions are marked below. Each is within an ellipse, a parallelogram, a cup shape and a rectangle.

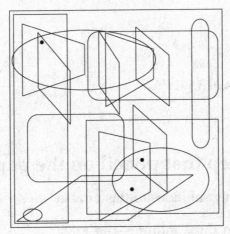

A175. Straight from the horse's mouth (Q135)

The ten words for a horse are: SHIRE, GELDING, PALFREY, STALLION, CHARGER, STEED, FILLY, COLT, COB, and NAG.

A176. I, thief, confess (Q126)

I had stolen . . . . a kiss!

A177. Finding an old friend unexpectedly (Q107)

The missing figure is '1'. Reading across the rows and continuing downwards from row to row there are successively closer and closer approximations to the digits of our old friend π; thus:

3
3.1
3.14
3.141
3.1415
3.14159
3.141592
3.1 the start of 3.1415926

A178. Keep that pencil on the paper (Q118)

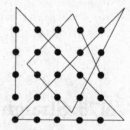

There are many solutions to this puzzle. Here is Kwizzer's:

It took him three minutes and eight seconds. James Riddell, seeing he was behind, hurled his pencil from him. 'An obvious put-up job contrived by that dishonest clown,' he roared, 'with whose name my lips will not be sullied.' Then he pushed his way through the delighted, laughing crowd to the door.

It did not make the columns, being pushed off by a major story, but all apart from Riddell enjoyed the scene.

A179. Get this square (Q127)

B	O	R	E	D
O	L	I	V	E
R	I	P	E	N
E	V	E	N	S
D	E	N	S	E

because unripe

A180. Extra-terrestrial aliens exposed (Q180)

The false assumption Lady Pamela had suggested was one of scale. The experts had assumed that the aliens were corporeal, solid beings – comparable in size to human beings or their own robots.

What had come to earth, controlling a vast army of robots, was not a group or a tribe of animal-like creatures but a vast colony of collectively intelligent microbes. Billions of microscopic creatures with an intricate but imperceptibly faint radio intercommunication system formed an intelligent single whole – a great and very powerful brain.

The colony was of monstrous collective intelligence but in size and form the units which acted as neurons were single, free-living protozoa. The aliens were what we would call a very large scattered colony of bacteria. No-one had been looking at the Putney house or its surroundings for micro-organisms tactically scattered around the area.

The colonies had evolved on Mars but now lived in tiny meteorite-spaceships all over the solar system. They had developed collective intelligence and the ability to parasitise any complex information system, including the human brain. They had been sending out undetectably minute signals and through the scattered chain of minute amplifiers which their robots had laid over a wide area were able to penetrate the computer and telephone network and thus control the way people thought and behaved.

The more intelligent the system, the better they were able to control it. This is why they were so afraid of less intelligent people.

The Professor's team found them and soon discovered the antiseptic combination of liquid and fumes that wiped them out.

I do not suppose that you will have guessed all that fantasy, but if you guessed that they were too small to be found you can count yourself as having solved this puzzle.